THE
CONSPIRACY
FILES

THE
CONSPIRACY
FILES

HISTORY'S GREATEST
SECRETS REVEALED

LEO MOYNIHAN

NEW BURLINGTON

This edition first published in 2021 by
New Burlington Books,
The Old Brewery, 6 Blundell Street,
London N7 9BH, United Kingdom.

ISBN 978-1-80242-015-9

Conceived, designed, and produced by
The Bright Press, an imprint of the Quarto Group,
The Old Brewery, 6 Blundell Street,
London N7 9BH, United Kingdom.
T (0)20 7700 6700
www.QuartoKnows.com

PUBLISHER: James Evans
EDITORIAL DIRECTOR: Isheeta Mustafi
ART DIRECTOR: James Lawrence
MANAGING EDITOR: Jacqui Sayers
COMMISSIONING EDITOR: Abbie Sharman
PROJECT EDITOR: Richard Webb
DESIGN: Ginny Zeal

Printed in Singapore

10 9 8 7 6 5 4 3 2 1

Cover picture: Shutterstock

CONTENTS

Introduction **6**

INTRODUCTION

In May 2011, President Barack Obama made an address to the White House Correspondents' Association dinner. He started with, "My *fellow* Americans," with an ironic emphasis on "fellow," a riposte to the recent conspiracy theory that he was not born in the United States, and therefore not a legitimate president.

In the audience that night was Donald Trump, a loud believer in the theory, but with Obama's birth certificate recently proving it to be false, the president went on to mock his doubter-in-chief. "I know that he's taken some flack lately—no one is prouder to put this birth certificate matter to rest than the Donald. And that's because he can finally get back to the issues that matter, like did we fake the Moon landing? What really happened in Roswell? And—where are Biggie and Tupac?" It was a brilliant retort, bringing wild laughter in the room and online sites alike, but five years later, Trump himself would take the front door keys to the White House from Obama. Much of the support he garnered and the "fake news" he advocated proved that, within politics and the modern world as a whole, there is still very much an appetite for questioning the status quo. Conspiracy theories remain as prevalent today as they ever have.

In *The Conspiracy Files* we delve into that fascination, looking closely at the theories that continue to intrigue and anger those who believe in them. By definition, a conspiracy theory is the belief that powerful but covert groups are responsible for an unresolved event or phenomenon, with sinister motives and often harmful consequences. These theories have become more widespread in recent years with the advent of the Internet, but they have always been around. In this book we will look back at historic examples such as the widely held belief that Jesus was married and perhaps even had children, and that Adolf Hitler faked his death and lived out his life in South America.

We have been intrigued by fame and celebrity throughout history, so theories surrounding the rich and famous will always be popular. In these pages we will examine conspiracies concerning eminent glitterati such as Princess Diana, Elvis Presley, and Marilyn Monroe. Less glamorous but equally compelling are the powerful secrets kept from us in the darkest stretches of the world's corridors of power. From North and South America to Australia, we examine the suspicious fate of leaders (both political and criminal) such as John F. Kennedy, Pablo Escobar, and Harold Holt.

We also look closely at the alleged sinister cover-ups that continue to interest and enrage theorists, from the strange case in France in the 1950s that saw almost a whole village suffer a mass poisoning with psychotic consequences, or the very recent belief that the Covid-19 pandemic was in fact purposefully engineered.

Some you may believe, some you may not, but one thing is certain, *The Conspiracy Files* are open and they certainly are fascinating.

Did the US spacecraft Apollo 11 really land on the Moon in 1969 or were the pictures faked as part of an audacious lunar cover-up?

1

THE RICH AND FAMOUS

We only ever get to see the premieres, the gigs, and the expensive gowns, so it is little wonder that we have long had a fascination with the rich and famous, and what really goes on in their lives away from the flashing bulbs. In this chapter we will look at Brazil's Ronaldo, the best soccer player on the planet at the time—was he forced to play in the 1998 World Cup final by his sportswear brand? Are The Beatles not quite what they seem and was the eventual killing of Osama bin Laden—at one point the most famous (and wanted) man on Earth—all that the US government had us believe?

THE
DEATH OF
DIANA

THE CONSPIRACY: .... PRINCESS DIANA
                                      WAS MURDERED

LOCATION: .... PARIS, FRANCE

DATE: .... AUGUST 31, 1997

A sea of flowers stretches out from Kensington Palace in London, once
the home of Princess Diana, but now deep in mourning. Strangers
console one another in a unifying show of unparalleled grief. All over
the world, a public touched by a very modern royal share a global
outpouring of love and heartache. The death of Diana, Princess of
Wales, in a car crash in Paris on a warm summer's night in 1997 was a
devastating loss to so many who felt they knew her. However, with that
affection came also a deep sense of anger and suspicion toward those
they held responsible.

A quarter of a century after the fatal accident, there are many who
remain wholly unconvinced that this was an *accident* at all, and despite
an inquiry looking closely at what went on that night, suspicion and
mistrust remain as potent as that original show of love and grief.

By the summer of 1997, Princess Diana (born Lady Diana Spencer) seemed to be in a happy place, a new upturn in her largely troubled and hugely public life. Since the breakdown of her marriage to the future king of England five years earlier, Diana had struggled to find peace, but now, desperate to keep her two boys out of the spotlight and to offer some sort of normality to their lives, it looked from the outside as if she had found her own happiness in the limelight.

In 1995 Diana had done a television interview with the BBC's *Panorama* show in which she, in no uncertain terms, put across her side of the marriage to Prince Charles, admitting that it had been "a crowded" one, due to her husband's love for another woman, Camilla Parker-Bowles. But two years later, her divorce finalized, free from official royal "duties" but still able to influence the world (her recent anti-landmine campaign was a huge success), Diana was enjoying her first public relationship since Charles. She and Dodi

A princess alone, but Diana was in a happy place in the weeks before her tragic accident.

Al-Fayed, the son of the billionaire Egyptian businessman Mohamed Al-Fayed, were being photographed (the paparazzi were never far from Diana's movements) and were definitely an item.

On the morning of August 30, 1997, Diana was photographed on Dodi's father's yacht off Sardinia. Lying on deck together, this seemed to be the start of a new, loving chapter in a turbulent life story. The couple embraced, Diana sat at the boat's bow, her legs hanging off the edge in a show of contentment.

The next night, those pictures now adorning the covers of most of the world's newspapers, Diana and Dodi left the Ritz in Paris in a car driven by the hotel's head of security. As ever they were pursued by eager paparazzi, but this time, what turned into a car chase through the city ended in tragedy when their car crashed in a tunnel, killing the couple and their driver.

The wreck of the
Mercedes W140 in
the Pont de l'Alma
tunnel in Paris.

A CONSPIRACY

The immediate anger after Diana's death was geared toward the photographers who had chased the car, looking for another photo that the world would be eager to see. There was a sense that photographers had for too long made Diana's life a misery, and some went even as far as to argue that the paparazzi had organized the chase and made sure it was fatal. That they sought and got one final snap.

But, in time, more grievous claims were made elsewhere; even Mohamed Al-Fayed stated that he felt that this was far from an accident, that in fact institutions far more powerful than mere photographers had been behind the death of his son and the princess. Al-Fayed went public, saying Diana was pregnant with Dodi's child, going on to say that the royal family "could not accept that an Egyptian Muslim could eventually be the stepfather of the future King of England," and that the establishment had plotted the accident, even having her body embalmed immediately to hide the pregnancy.

The establishment, the royal family, Britain's security services; this was a concentrated effort from all of them to kill off Diana. It was said that the driver, Henri Paul, was in fact working for Britain's MI6. Background checks showed his personal wealth was far more than that of a security chief at a Paris hotel, and then there was the claim after his autopsy that he had been drinking and that influenced the reckless way he was driving.

French investigators reported that Paul was three times over the French legal drink-driving limit, but this was challenged by his employer, Al-Fayed, who hired a pathologist to counter the claims, arguing that his demeanor on the CCTV footage that night was not in line with a drunk man. Suspicious of the official findings, some have argued that those responsible for the deaths swapped Paul's body for someone they knew would show high levels of alcohol in his blood.

Many of those who suspect foul play point to the car itself, arguing that the Mercedes they were driving had been tampered with and that malfunction at high speed had caused the accident. It is a theory that is consistent with another argument that stated Diana herself was scared for her life and she had declared real concerns for her safety. Years after her death Diana's former butler, Paul Burrell, disclosed a letter she'd written. In it she said, "I am sitting here at my desk today in October, longing for someone to hug me and encourage me to keep strong and hold my head high. This particular phase in my life is the most dangerous." Diana went on to say (the name was withheld) "... is planning 'an accident' in my car, brake failure and serious head injury in order to make the path clear for Charles to marry."

Further suspicions were raised by the fact that Diana and Dodi weren't wearing seat belts. It is said that Diana was always strict about wearing a belt and that her fears for her safety would surely have meant she did that night. Professor André Lienhart, who reviewed the emergency services' response for the French government investigation of the incident, went on to say that had they been wearing belts, "... we'd have been able to save her."

Prince Charles with his young sons, Prince William and Prince Harry, inspecting the sea of flowers left by a mourning nation.

Diana's security guard, Trevor
Rees-Jones (left), and the driver,
Henri Paul, leaving the Ritz in
Paris. Rees-Jones was the only
survivor of the crash.

THE SKEPTICS

The hysteria that surrounded the death of Diana and the many wild accusations
that followed was enough for skeptics to distrust the notion of a planned
killing. Some said that the world's florists had hatched the plan to sell more
flowers or that Diana and Dodi faked their deaths to live quietly outside of the
limelight. Surely any "serious" claims were as nonsensical as those?

There was also Operation Paget, an inquiry set up in 2004 by the British police
to investigate conspiracy theories surrounding Diana's death, looking closely
and publicly at every aspect of the incident. Suggestions that she was pregnant
were found to be unreliable; friends giving evidence stated that she was using
contraception and that close confidantes would have known, and it was argued
that her quick embalming was due to the August heat in Paris.

The official line that the driver had been drunk was backed up by further tests
taken on blood and eye samples, and it was argued that Paul was in fact a
long-time alcoholic and was therefore able to hide any signs of drinking.
Operation Paget was also given unprecedented access to the files of MI5 and
MI6, and went on to conclude that there was no link to Paul with any of the
security services. In 2008, the jury's final verdict was "unlawful killing" by the
driver and the pursuing photographers.

THE
BEATLES
IMPOSTER

THE CONSPIRACY: ....PAUL MCCARTNEY DIED
AND WAS REPLACED BY A BODY DOUBLE

LOCATION: .... LONDON, ENGLAND

DATE: .... NOVEMBER 1966

On November 9, 1966, aged just twenty-four, Paul McCartney died.
Just months after The Beatles' last ever concert, and weeks before the
band from Liverpool in northern England would start to record their
eighth album, *Sgt. Pepper's Lonely Hearts Club Band*, McCartney was
killed in a car crash. However, to avoid the terrible grief that this would
cause their devoted fans, the band kept his death a secret, replaced him
with a body double, and continued to enchant the world with their
music. It's a theory that captured the imagination of fans, spreading
like wildfire and attracting enormous interest.

PAUL'S RISE AND (APPARENT) FALL

By the fall of 1966, Paul McCartney, John Lennon, George Harrison, and Ringo Starr—The Beatles—were the biggest thing on the planet. "We're more popular than Jesus," John had infamously said. Since forming in Liverpool, with their brand of "Mersey Beat" sweeping the globe, they had released seven albums, topped the charts countless times, and had planned a new groundbreaking album that would change music forever. But then some fans started to listen more carefully, and clues to a secret started to unravel. Clues that led to an idea that started to spread. "Paul is dead."

In October 1969, a DJ on a radio show in Detroit started a discussion. An article in a student newspaper weeks earlier had run with the headline, "Is Paul McCartney Dead?" citing clues in their recent music that suggested he was. "Turn me on, dead man," could be heard if the intro on "Revolution 9" from *The White Album* was played backward. On further inspection, it was found that at the end of "Strawberry Fields," Lennon sings, "I buried Paul." The world began to listen.

There were visual clues on album covers; clues that proved the band's living members felt such guilt for the cover up that they wanted (even if only subliminally) to unburden themselves. Take the iconic *Abbey Road* album cover (released shortly after the rumors began) in which the members of the band are walking over a marked crosswalk. The cover represents a funeral procession. Lennon is in white, the heavenly figure; Starr in black, the mortician; Harrison is in denim, the gravedigger, and McCartney is barefooted—the corpse. McCartney is also out of step with the others, and holding a cigarette in his right hand, despite being left-handed. The white Volkswagen Beetle in the background has the number plate that reads "LMW 28IF." LMW stands for Linda McCartney Weeps and the 28IF represents the age McCartney would have been *if* he had been alive when the picture was taken.

The track "I Am The Walrus" from the earlier album *Magical Mystery Tour* also attracted close scrutiny. A (false) rumor started that walrus is Greek for corpse. Lyrics such as "Waiting for the van to come" and "Pretty little policemen" allude to McCartney's accident, while the opening line "I am he as you are he as you are me and we are all together" suggests the whole band being in on the conspiracy. The song ends with a live BBC broadcast of

Shakespeare's *King Lear*, in which Oswald groans, "O, untimely death!" and in another song, "Glass Onion," Lennon sings, "Here's another clue for you all / The Walrus was Paul."

And so, the rumors persisted. Apparently McCartney had left the Abbey Road studios having argued with his band members, and driving too fast, he had crashed and died. It was said that McCartney was officially pronounced dead (O.P.D.) at 5 a.m. On the *Sgt. Pepper* album cover, he is wearing a sewn-on patch on his uniform. It says "O.P.D."

With the support of Britain's security service (M15), the surviving members of the band and their management, very much concerned for the overwhelming grief the news would cause, chose to replace Paul with a lookalike from Edinburgh, an orphan called Billy Sheers, who learned to sing, talk, and act like the original.

The Volkswagen Beetle with its prophetic number plate, which can been seen on the cover of the Abbey Road album.

Paul McCartney
performing later
in life. Or is it?

THE SKEPTICS

Despite the elaborate nature of the rumors, they soon took hold. A television special ran in New York, interviewing the writer Fred LaBour who had written an article in *The Michigan Daily* headlined "McCartney Dead; New Evidence Brought to Light," which further fueled the flames. LaBour is said to have stated it was only supposed to be a joke, but so enthralled was the world that the band's press office had to release a statement denying it as "a load of rubbish," and McCartney himself appeared on the cover of *Life Magazine* with his wife, Linda, and their kids under the banner "Paul is still with us." Sales of Beatles records rocketed!

As for those clues in their lyrics, John Lennon was always puzzled by the fascination in hidden meanings to the words he wrote, and later said that he often purposefully wrote obscure and enigmatic lyrics to confuse and intrigue. It certainly worked.

The band broke up in 1970. It is interesting that on the night McCartney was supposed to have died, November 9, 1966, Lennon met his future wife, Yoko Ono, a relationship that many suggest caused the death of The Beatles. Perhaps an omen?

As for McCartney, he could later laugh at his apparent demise, taking a jibe at the "Paul is Dead" statement when he called his 1993 album "Paul is Live."

ELVIS LIVES!

THE CONSPIRACY: .... ELVIS PRESLEY
FAKED HIS DEATH

LOCATION: .... MEMPHIS, TENNESSEE,
UNITED STATES

DATE: .... AUGUST 16, 1977

The King is dead... Long live the King. But what if the King didn't die? What if the King, the one and only Elvis Presley, faked his own death and disappeared to live a long and quiet life away from all the fame and consequence that his music had given him? From breaking onto the rock 'n' roll scene in the mid-1950s, Elvis Presley was arguably the most recognizable man on Earth, his songs were played on radio stations from Memphis to Melbourne, his costumes revered, and every inch of his life scrutinized.

On August 16, 1977, fans around the world mourned the passing of their King, but ever since that day sightings of Elvis very much alive and well have been reported. Of course, his music lived on, but what if he did too?

ELVIS COMES TO HIS THRONE

On Elvis's eleventh birthday in 1946, he unwrapped a present from his devoted mother, Gladys. It was a gift that would change the world. It was his first guitar. The Second World War was not long over and what would follow was years of hardship, rebuilding, and austerity, but as a young Elvis mastered his new "toy," bringing a revolutionary sound to a new, young audience, nothing would be the same again.

From the moment Elvis's first hit "That's Alright" aired in 1954, he was a star. The way he sang enthralled a generation, the way he moved shocked their parents. Charismatic, talented, and handsome, Elvis and his phenomenon grew and grew. His sound, so influenced by the gospel music his mother used to play to him but with a modern and sexy edge, filled the airwaves. He was a regular on new television shows, and wherever he went he was mobbed by adoring and in some cases, obsessed fans. A stint in the army didn't dampen Elvis's fame. An equally successful transition into the world of cinema further reinforced his position as a global superstar, while later in his career his shows in Vegas were watched by thousands, and the iconic, bejeweled outfits he wore on stage became the uniform for millions of impersonators.

Elvis burst onto the scene in the 1950s, becoming the most famous man on the planet.

Even his home was famous. Graceland in Memphis became a mecca for Elvis fans, and it was from there, on an August morning in 1977, the news came that Elvis was dead, at only forty-two years old. For hoards of devoted followers, the truth was too hard to bear.

SUSPICIOUS MINDS

The medical examiner's official cause of death was "hypertensive heart disease associated with atherosclerotic heart disease," but the death certificate was kept private and won't be made public until 2027, fifty years after Elvis's death. This is merely Tennessee state law, but immediately there were those who suspected a cover up. Then, on the very day he was said to have died, a man resembling Elvis was reported to have been boarding a flight from Memphis airport to Argentina, under the name John Burrows, a pseudonym used by Elvis when checking into hotels.

Two days later, there was a funeral at Graceland. But it was an event that only fueled the flames for those refusing to believe Elvis had gone. The huge copper coffin was so heavy that the pallbearers struggled to carry it, not because Elvis had put on so much weight, but because this was a special coffin designed to keep the wax dummy inside cool on a hot August day. It didn't work.

Elvis's home, Graceland, has remained a tourist attraction since his supposed death in 1977.

Elvis's grave at his home in Graceland. To some, the misspelling of his middle name is a clue to the theory that he never died.

Photos of the open casket aroused further suspicion and many observers noticed that Elvis's forehead had beads of sweat, in keeping with an overheated waxwork. Gene Smith, a cousin of Elvis, noted that, "His nose looked kinda puggy-looking, and his right sideburn was sticking straight out—it looked about an inch... And his hairline looked like a hairpiece or something was glued on."

On the headstone, Elvis's full name is written as ELVIS AARON PRESLEY, but his middle name was originally spelled Aron and so again, those who believed his death was faked took this as a message from Elvis himself to his fans that he was in fact alive.

WHY WOULD HE FAKE HIS OWN DEATH?

Most of those people who deny Elvis died that day in 1977 point to how difficult the singer had begun to find the all-consuming levels of fame in his life. His health had suffered and by faking his death, and moving abroad, Elvis could live out his life in peace. It is said that he cashed three life insurance policies prior to his death, netting nearly $2 million.

However, others think there was a shadier side to his decision. Gail Brewer-Giorgio, the author of the 1988 book, *Elvis is Alive*, states that the singer had become an informant for the FBI, helping to bring down a Mafia organization called "The Fraternity" and, with the criminal underground discovering he was a mole, was forced into a witness protection program. The safest thing to do was to fake his death.

IS THAT THE KING?

From that early sighting of Elvis at Memphis airport, sightings of him living out his life have been as regular as his hit records. The New Year's Eve after his death, Mike Joseph, a visitor to Graceland (now a major tourist attraction) took a photo of his hero's pool house. On closer inspection, he noticed a figure at a window, and with a magnifying glass noticed that the figure looked remarkably like Elvis. In 1984, a photo of the preacher Jesse Jackson, Muhammad Ali, and a man uncannily resembling Elvis stirred suspicions. The sports promoter Larry Kolb said it was him with his client, Ali, but the boxer disagreed. "That's my friend, Elvis," he said in an interview.

Most sightings have been of Elvis buying burgers or filling his car with gas, but perhaps the strangest came in the 1990 movie, *Home Alone*. A scene in the movie shows the mother of the boy left at home, at an airport remonstrating with an airline official. Behind her in a line of people is a bearded man, a mere bit part actor, but to a keen eye it does look like an aging Elvis, who did after all love the movies.

Today, Elvis would be deep into his eighties, but sightings continue. Close to home (literally) was the video in 2016 that showed an elderly white-haired and bearded man, working as a groundskeeper at Graceland. Might Elvis, having lived his life away from the limelight, finally come home? Over two million people have viewed the video on YouTube, proving that whether he lived or died, Elvis's fame is still intact.

Elvis Presley remains as iconic today as ever; to many, the King will never die.

THE SKEPTICS

Such is the belief (or is it hope?) among those who argue that Elvis did not die in 1977 that many have felt compelled to debunk each argument they might make. For example, it would not have been possible for Elvis to fly to Argentina on the day of his supposed death as international flights didn't leave Memphis back then. The middle name on his gravestone, Aaron, was actually Elvis's preferred spelling as many legal documents attest to; the extra in *Home Alone* was a close friend of the director who appeared in several of his movies, and the 2016 video of the Graceland groundkeeper is in fact a man called Bill Barmer, much smaller than Elvis and a long-time employee there.

It seems theories about Elvis's death will never subside. Such was the love his fans had for him, such was their devotion, it's no surprise that so many refuse to believe that Elvis ever left the building.

THE NIKE
CONSPIRACY

THE CONSPIRACY: .... NIKE INFLUENCED
BRAZIL'S SELECTION OF RONALDO
FOR THE 1998 WORLD CUP

LOCATION: .... PARIS, FRANCE

DATE: .... JULY 12, 1998

It was the biggest match in soccer, and he was the best player in the world. Ronaldo, a twenty-one-year-old goal scorer from Rio de Janeiro had lit up the 1998 World Cup, scoring four goals on the way to helping Brazil reach the final. There they would face the hosts, France, whose team also had a number of superb players but none with the iconic status of Ronaldo. His face graced posters everywhere that summer; he was a darling of the sponsors, the most recognizable man on the planet. The sportswear giant, Nike, paid the Brazilian team and Ronaldo millions to wear their products. This was to be their night, as well as his.

But, when the team-sheets were handed in, Ronaldo's name was missing and the world gasped. Half an hour before kick-off a new team-sheet emerged from Brazil's locker room, this time with his name on it. Something was wrong. France won the game 3–0, but for many in soccer-crazy Brazil it looked like a cover up, and they had strong suspicions that Nike was behind it.

A NEW SUPERSTAR

In 1996, Nike made a television advert. In it, they showed an incredible goal scored by Ronaldo for Barcelona, the Spanish team he played for at the time. Ronaldo picked the ball up on the halfway line, before taking it around five opponents, and scoring a goal that had the world purring. *"Imagine you asked God to be the best player in the world, and he listened to you,"* was the line over the advertisement's footage, and it underlined just how highly the young player was regarded.

Bursting on to the scene with Brazilian club, Cruzeiro, Ronaldo came to Europe in 1994, scoring goal after goal for PSV Eindhoven, Barcelona, and then Inter Milan prior to the 1998 World Cup, generating world-record transfer fees as he went. In 1996, Nike and the Brazilian Football Confederation signed a contract worth $100 million. Nike would manufacture Brazil's kit and be a cosponsor of the team in what was the largest-ever deal for a national side. In the same year, the American sportswear brand also signed Ronaldo. He would wear Nike boots and appear in their adverts in a ten-year deal worth $180 million. The World Cup was around the corner and Nike had soccer's most iconic country and the greatest player in the world on their books.

In 1998, Ronaldo was the most famous footballer on Earth.

THE FINAL

On the day of the World Cup final, the Brazilian team, favorites to beat their hosts, France, enjoyed lunch at Chateâu de Grande Romaine in Lésigny, near Paris, before going to their rooms for an afternoon nap.

All eyes were on Ronaldo but before he could enjoy a rest in the confines of his hotel room, he suffered a fit. He was convulsing violently and frothing at the mouth. His roommate Roberto Carlos cried for help; teammates came. His fellow striker Edmundo said, "When I saw what it was, I despaired. It was a really strong and shocking scene." One player administered first-aid, making sure their star teammate didn't swallow his tongue, before the team's doctors treated him and got him into bed where he slept. They vigilantly watched over him and contemplated not telling him what had happened but were advised by some of the players that they must. Ronaldo was concerned on hearing the news and agreed to leave for the hospital in Paris for some tests. The rest of the squad left for the stadium.

For the manager, Mario Zágallo, this was very far from the ideal preparation for a final; worried about his striker's health, he picked his team. Ronaldo was left out. The media couldn't believe it; Brazilian fans hearing the news were distraught. But not for long. Thirty minutes before kick-off, Brazil released a second team-sheet; this time Ronaldo was in. He played but he was subdued, unable to make his usual mark on the game and the French were victorious.

When the Brazil team returned from Paris, they were greeted with disdain by a country that felt they had sold out and were far too influenced by their big sponsors. There was even a parliamentary inquiry into Nike's influence as many suggested that on seeing the original team-sheet they had demanded that Ronaldo play, that they had it written in a contract and there was no way their star player could miss the biggest game of them all.

Despair: as the French
celebrated, an out-of-
sorts Ronaldo was left
to wonder, "What if...?"

THE SKEPTICS

While plenty of soccer fans have lamented the role of big sponsors in the game, the inquiry in Brazil could find no wrongdoing from Nike. Ronaldo himself was a star witness, and reiterated that on getting the all-clear at the hospital, he arrived at the stadium and pleaded with his manager that he was in fact OK, and fit enough to play.

The manager was concerned, as was the team doctor, but in the end, how could they leave out the most famous player on the planet? "Imagine if I stopped him playing and Brazil lost," the doctor later said. "At that moment I'd have to go and live on the North Pole."

MARILYN
MONROE

THE CONSPIRACY: .... THE ACTRESS WAS MURDERED

LOCATION: ....LOS ANGELES, CALIFORNIA, UNITED STATES

DATE: .... AUGUST 4, 1962

Marilyn Monroe was a personality that embodied Hollywood style and glamour. Her name remains synonymous with red carpets, award ceremonies, and lavish gowns. She was an actress who captured the hearts of a generation of movie-goers, drawn to her soft tone, her playful, comedic manner, her musicality, and of course her unique beauty. The peroxide-blonde hair, the deep red lips that matched the carpets on which she walked—Marilyn Monroe seemed to have it all. Until she had nothing. Her death in 1962 shocked the world. All everyone saw was that seductive image, the magazine covers, and the jewels; but the world was left mourning a woman who needed friends more than the diamonds she famously sang about.

The official line was that this was suicide, an overdose taken by a lonely and depressed woman; but very quickly more probing questions began to be asked, and soon after came the suspicions. Was this really suicide, and if not, who had killed Marilyn?

A STAR IS BORN

In 1946, a red-haired, hard-working model called Norma Jeane Mortenson sat in an office with a Twentieth Century Fox film executive. She had been given a screen test and although not overly enthusiastic, the Hollywood studio offered her a contract. But the name... that would have to change. Marilyn Miller was a popular old Broadway star. Monroe was her mother's maiden name. A star was born.

The studios worked with Monroe, who was shy and a little insecure, coming up with a change in image. The hair went from red to peroxide blonde, and in time she began to get major film roles followed by acclaim, recognition, and ultimately fame. By 1953, she was a certified and very bankable star. Movies such as *Niagara* and *Gentlemen Prefer Blondes* set the tone and by the end of the 1950s, she was arguably the world's most famous actress, gaining critical acclaim for performances in huge hits such as *Some Like it Hot*.

The young Marilyn Monroe quickly began to charm her audience.

Behind the scenes, fame came at a cost. There were marriages to high-profile stars; the baseball player, Joe DiMaggio and then the playwright Arthur Miller. Neither lasted. Old nude photos resurfaced causing further scandal, and the constant scrutiny of her performances, love life, and image had taken its toll. She had been treated for depression. With a history of mental health issues in her family, Monroe had sought psychiatric help, checking into the Payne Whitney Hospital for treatment. She continued to get help from Dr. Ralph Greenson, and by the summer of 1962 she seemed to be happy, looking forward to new beginnings, not troubled pasts.

Recently divorced from Miller, Monroe had bought herself a new $75,000 house in the upmarket LA neighborhood of Brentwood, she was on the cover of *Life* magazine, a shoot with *Paris Match* was scheduled, and she had been re-hired (her previously erratic behavior had seen her fired) for the movie *Something's Got to Give*. It is said she was planning a press conference, one in which she would announce a new start.

On August 5, 1962, Marilyn Monroe was found face down, nude, on her bed, with empty bottles of prescription pills around her. Suicide...

Monroe's bedroom on the morning after her death in 1962.

Just three months before her death, Marilyn celebrated the birthday of President Kennedy (right) and his brother Robert. She was romantically linked to both men.

... OR MURDER?

Almost two weeks after her death, the Chief Coroner, Theodore Curphey, classified Monroe's death as "probable suicide." The word "probable" was always going to raise suspicions. The autopsy showed she had died from acute barbiturate poisoning, consistent with the pills she had been prescribed by her doctor. Plenty of evidence pointed to her recent mental state, her doctors were interviewed and confirmed her fragility, but for others it didn't seem right; many believed Monroe had turned a corner, and surely she would have written a note if she planned to kill herself?

And then there was her private life; a private life that involved people far from the West Coast glitz of Hollywood, closer to the East Coast political hub of Washington DC. Rumors of an affair with President John F. Kennedy began to surface. Monroe had seductively sung *Happy Birthday* to him less than three months prior to her death, but it is believed that while they did have an affair, it was very brief and meant little to either of them.

It was the far more serious affair with the president's brother, the US Attorney General Robert Kennedy, that many felt was the more suspicious. It fueled the first conspiracy theories that Monroe's death was not her own doing. In 1973, the writer Norman Mailer published *Marilyn: A Biography* in which he repeated the rumor of their affair and stated that the FBI or the CIA had had the actress killed, in order to create a "point of pressure… against the Kennedys."

It wasn't the first time the relationship with Robert had been linked to her death. In 1964, a pamphlet written by anti-communist Frank Capell named *The Strange Death of Marilyn Monroe* went one step further saying that Robert, threatened by Monroe's intention to go public with the affair and cause a scandal, ordered her murder himself.

In October 2017, the JFK files were released. President Trump was privy to the classified papers and although much of the contents remained private due to national security concerns, a letter emerged from the FBI to Robert Kennedy saying that a new book was due to be written that would reveal details of the relationship.

Monroe's housekeeper, Eunice Murray, would reveal that Robert Kennedy visited Monroe on the night of her death, and Ted Landreth, the producer of a BBC documentary *The Last Days of Marilyn Monroe*, stated that Kennedy confirmed he was in LA that night, and he suspected they had had a big row. To further the theory that Monroe had simply got too close to those in power, a report was published claiming that she had kept a diary with notes on several internationally sensitive issues. It included a plan to kill Cuban leader, Fidel Castro, plus intimate details about her love affairs with both the Kennedy brothers. Many believed she was prepared to go public with it all.

John Miner, the head of the Los Angles District Attorney's medical-legal office when Monroe died, years later admitted to seeing transcripts of tapes of Monroe talking to her psychiatrist, Dr. Gleeson, not long before her death. He said this was a buoyant, upbeat woman talking freely and candidly about her life. "There was no possible way this woman could have killed herself," Miner said. "She had very specific plans for her future. She knew exactly what she wanted to do."

Marilyn embodied
Hollywood glamour, but
behind the lipstick
and mascara was a sad
and lonely superstar.

THE SKEPTICS

Despite the affairs with America's most powerful men, and the political dangers that might have come with them, Monroe's mental state remains the firmest clue to what happened to her, and those who are skeptical that foul play was involved point to the fact that she wasn't well, that she drank alcohol with pills, that she had attempted suicide before, and was depressed about her fame and numerous failed relationships.

Frank Capell's theories were seen simply as coming from a staunch anti-communist who believed the Kennedys were dangerous, and the tapes that John Miner spoke of were of interest—but because Dr. Gleeson had reportedly destroyed them and was now dead himself, it was only ever Miner's word that they even existed. It seems that Monroe's death will remain as a "probable suicide," and that her life will forever be defined by both glamour and sadness.

TUPAC SHAKUR'S DEATH

THE CONSPIRACY: .... THE RAPPER TUPAC
SHAKUR FAKED HIS OWN DEATH

LOCATION: ....LAS VEGAS, NEVADA,
UNITED STATES

DATE: ....SEPTEMBER 13, 1996

The hip-hop star Tupac Shakur lay dead on his hospital bed. He had
suffered four bullet wounds in a drive-by shooting in Las Vegas, one
of which pierced his lung. He was just twenty-five years old.

Having made four platinum albums prior to his death, Tupac was one
of the most successful musicians of any genre and a major influence in
the world of rap. But his legacy didn't die with him; it grew. There were
seven more platinum albums released posthumously. Tupac was still
big business, with an army of fans hungry to know more about his
turbulent life—and his supposed death. It wasn't long after that night
in Vegas that rumors surfaced. Rumors that soon turned into
conspiracy theories.

THE BACKGROUND

In November 1991, Tupac Shakur's debut album was released. *2Pacalypse Now* was a massive hit, inspiring the likes of Eminem and Nas, but it was also his first brush with controversy; even US Vice-President Dan Quayle weighed in, arguing that its provocative lyrics had "no place in our society."

While hip-hop musicians continue to cause contention and upset authority figures, through the early 1990s the genre was arguably the most successful on the planet, and right at the top of the tree was Tupac Shakur. However, controversy and violence shadowed his career. In late 1994, Tupac was imprisoned for sexual assault, but having seen his $1.4 million bond paid by Death Row Records' CEO Suge Knight, he was forced to sign with them.

With financial problems hovering over him, it is said that Tupac wrote a letter to a magazine editor, talking of starting a "new chapter." Having interviewed him, one music journalist commented that Tupac's personality had fundamentally changed since his imprisonment, that he was more aggressive; he "seemed like a completely transformed person."

Prior to his death, Tupac had become one of the biggest names in music.

TUPAC'S DEATH

On the night Tupac was supposedly shot, he had attended the big Mike
Tyson heavyweight bout at Las Vegas' MGM Grand hotel with Suge Knight
and an entourage of associates. After the fight, he was involved in a fracas
with a known gang member called Orlando "Baby Lane" Anderson, a member
of LA's Southside Crips. One of the entourage accused him of a previous
robbery, which led to Tupac punching Anderson before several of his
associates joined in the attack on the solo gang member. Shortly afterward,
Tupac was in his BMW, followed by his entourage, when at a stop light a
white Cadillac Sedan pulled up alongside him and an occupant fired into his
car. He was hit once in his arm, once in his thigh, and twice in his chest.
Knight escaped with injuries from shards of glass. Tupac's bodyguard was
in one of the other cars, driving the star's girlfriend.

Six days later, having been put in an induced coma and on life-support,
Tupac Shakur was pronounced dead, officially due to respiratory failure
and cardiac arrest brought on by a severe loss of blood when his lung
was removed.

Tupac with
Suge Knight,
the CEO of
Death Row
records, who
benefited
financially
from the
star's
"death."

Tupac's aunt Assata
Shakur was given
political asylum
in Cuba. Is that why
he allegedly faked
his death and
moved there?

THE CONSPIRACY

It wasn't long before questions were being asked. Firstly because it wasn't long before Tupac was cremated in (what some people thought) a very low-key funeral. Suge Knight reportedly paid $3 million for the quick ceremony, the day after Tupac's death. Only he and the technician at the crematorium witnessed it. The technician (who then retired and has not been seen since) listed the body as measuring 6 feet and weighing 215 pounds. Tupac was 5 feet 10 and weighed 168 pounds. Later, a planned public memorial was canceled.

Doubts were raised about events on the night of the shooting. Tupac had been involved in shootings before, and death threats against him were nothing new. It was known that he was paranoid about his safety. Why then, when attending a very public event, had he not worn his bulletproof vest, and why had he asked his bodyguard and girlfriend to drive separately?

Did that "new chapter" Tupac had spoken of actually involve faking his death? Many believe that his new life is being lived in Cuba. Tupac's aunt, Assata Shakur, a member of the Black Liberation Army, was granted political asylum there in 1984. In 2010 hip-hop star Treach was asked if Shakur was really dead. "Last time I saw him he was in Cuba, man," he replied. Rapper Kendrick Lamar, in his 2017 track "Element" says, "Fake my death, go to Cuba, that's the only option." In 2018, photos were published that appeared to show Shakur partying with Rhianna on the island—as the trail of evidence continues, so the theory persists.

So much so, that a 2021 movie called *2Pac: The Great Escape from UMC* (University Medical Center in Vegas) states that Shakur, helped by Suge Knight, used a body double and actually left Las Vegas in a helicopter that night and relocated to Navajo tribal land in New Mexico where federal agents couldn't follow. The filmmaker, Rick Boss, claims to have got his information from Tupac's close family. "The family is aware of the movie and they're OK with the title so that should tell you more or less what's going on," Boss said.

Since his reported death, those who believe Tupac to be alive have sought and found clues that support their theory. For example, Tupac was a fan of the Italian Renaissance philosopher and politician Niccolò Machiavelli, who advocated faking his own death to gain an advantage over his enemies. Tupac's last album before the shooting was under the name Makaveli, a reference to his philosophical hero but also an anagram of "ALIVE K."

The streets of Havana in Cuba, the city where sightings of Tupac have intrigued those who suspect he's still alive.

THE SKEPTICS

Since his supposed death, Tupac Shakur has become even more successful than when he was alive. Most of the 75 million record sales were posthumous; his estate, ten years after his death, was worth more than that of Eminem or 50 Cent, and he remains so high profile that it is little wonder so many people believe (or want to believe) that Tupac never died.

Using technology and holograms, Tupac has appeared in a Snoop Dogg video and in 2012 he even headlined the huge Coachella festival in the United States, underlining his never-ending popularity and pulling power. Many simply feel this is down to clever marketing, that the myth of his faked death has fueled sales, and that keeping conspiracy theories and his legacy alive simply benefited the bank balance of Suge Knight and Death Row Records.

As for Tupac's supposed murder, no one was ever charged. Some have suggested it was New York gang members, possibly his friend-turned-rival Notorious B.I.G. (who was himself killed months later in what was speculated to be a revenge killing). Most of the witnesses stated that it was carried out by members of the Southside Crips gang in revenge for the assault on Anderson the same night. The *LA Times* in 2002 wrote that: "The shooting was carried out by a Compton gang called the Southside Crips to avenge the beating of one of its members by Shakur a few hours earlier. Orlando Anderson, the Crip whom Shakur had attacked, fired the fatal shots. Las Vegas police considered Anderson as a suspect and interviewed him only once, briefly. Anderson was killed nearly two years later in an unrelated gang shooting."

One of Tupac's infamous quotes was, "My only fear of death is reincarnation." Whatever the skeptics think, there are plenty of people who remain hopeful that could actually happen one day.

THE DEATH OF BRUCE LEE

THE CONSPIRACY: .... THE MARTIAL ARTS LEGEND WAS MURDERED

LOCATION: .... HONG KONG

DATE: .... JULY 20, 1973

On July 25, 1973, in Lake View Cemetery in Seattle, a funeral took place. Not the biggest, or the most lavish, but among the pallbearers carrying the coffin were a few well-known faces from the martial arts world and two leading members of the Hollywood glitterati, James Coburn and Steve McQueen.

Although over fifteen thousand mourners had turned out to pay their respects to Bruce Lee in Hong Kong, where he was already a huge star, he was still largely unknown to mainstream movie lovers in the United States. On that summer's day in Seattle, a group of family and friends mourned the death of this incredible young man, martial artist, and actor. However, very soon his name would be up in lights across the world and as Bruce Lee's fame spread, so did the suspicions about his sudden death at just thirty-two years old.

LEE'S RISE AND FALL

On August 19, 1973, a month after Bruce Lee's death, *Enter the Dragon* premiered in the United States and would go on to make $350 million worldwide, making its leading man a global star.

Bruce Lee was born in San Francisco in 1940 to Eurasian parents; the family moved to live in Hong Kong when he was just three months old. His father was an opera star and from a young age Bruce had stage and screen experience, but it was boxing and martial arts that took much of the young man's attention and time.

Moving back to the United States, Lee wanted to find a way of linking his love of kung fu with the movies. He got roles on US TV in the late 1960s, but was finding Hollywood a tougher nut to crack, so he returned to Hong Kong where he starred in several martial arts films that he hoped would garner attention from Hollywood studios. Movies such as *The Big Boss* in 1971 and then *Fist of Fury* a year later broke box office records across Asia, and so Warner Bros. offered Lee the lead role in *Enter the Dragon*. Suddenly kung fu was all the rage.

In May of 1973, two months before his death, Lee collapsed in Hong Kong suffering with severe headaches and seizures. Doctors diagnosed an excess of fluid on the brain. He was treated and returned home.

In July, after a number of meetings, Lee went to the home of Betty Ting Pei, a Taiwanese actress and Lee's mistress. There, Lee complained of

Lee with his mother, Grace, and his son, Brandon, photographed in 1970.

a headache and was given an Equagesic pill, which contained aspirin and a tranquilizer, before taking a nap. When he didn't return downstairs for dinner, Ting Pei went to his room, but couldn't wake him up; a doctor was called, they tried to resuscitate him but he was declared dead at Hong Kong's Queen Elizabeth Hospital.

"DEATH BY MISADVENTURE"

… That's what the official report said. It was stated that it was the aspirin in the pills Lee had taken that night that killed him, causing an allergic reaction, and another buildup of fluid on his brain. But, in time, other theories began to materialize. The cannabis he had been smoking might have proved fatal, or the muscle-relaxant medication he took for a back injury. Then there was the suggestion that due to having his underarm sweat glands removed, thinking sweat didn't look good on film, Lee had suffered from fatal heatstroke.

Some believed Bruce Lee's death was not health related at all. This was a thirty-two-year-old athlete, a man in his prime, a man who hardly drank, a man who ate all the right foods, and a man who constantly took health supplements.

But if it wasn't a reaction to medicine, what was it? The first rumor was that it was a prostitute acting in self-defense who killed Lee, when he became enraged after taking a natural but powerful aphrodisiac. Others pointed their fingers at his mistress, Betty Ting Pei, citing the fact that it was her who gave Lee his medicine and so had purposefully harmed him—an autopsy photo of Lee's bloated face suggested he had been poisoned. It was a rumor reinforced by the fact that Lee's business partner, trying to conceal the affair, had told the public that he had died at his house, not Ting Pei's.

Then there was talk of the Chinese Triads, a secret underground crime ring in Hong Kong, who wanted Lee dead due to business dealings they had with the actor. And even a supernatural theory that the Lee family had an evil curse set upon it, a speculation that became eerily relevant when Lee's son, Brandon, was shot and killed on the set of the 1994 movie, *The Crow*. Whatever happened to Lee, nothing seemed to add up and such was the need for his fans (Lee had a huge cult following) to get to the truth, it led to civil unrest.

Lee in his 1973 movie
Enter the Dragon, the
film that posthumously
made him a star.

THE SKEPTICS

Two years prior to his own death, Brandon Lee was asked about the many
theories that surrounded his father. He put it down to his legendary status.
"I think that's maybe why the rumors, which to me, are on the level of people
still talking about Elvis being alive, I think that's perhaps why so many of those
rumors sprung up—he was only thirty-two," he said.

2

POWERFUL SECRETS

Did you know that there is a conspiracy theory that it was actually America's Central Intelligence Agency that came up with the term "conspiracy theory" in 1967, as a way of discrediting the growing band of people who believed the government were lying about the assassination of President Kennedy? Could those in power be using that power for their own clandestine purposes? Here we look at those famous secrets such as an Illuminati controlling the world's affairs, and the age-old question of whether that world is, in fact, flat.

THE ASSASSINATION
OF JFK

THE CONSPIRACY: ....JFK WAS NOT KILLED
BY A LONE ASSASSIN

LOCATION: .. DALLAS, TEXAS, UNITED STATES

DATE: .... NOVEMBER 22, 1963

On the afternoon of November 22, 1963, an American soap opera called *As the World Turns* was interrupted by a news flash. Reports were coming in that shots had been fired at President John F. Kennedy. Over half an hour later, the news anchor Walter Cronkite was handed a piece of paper. Adjusting his glasses he said, "From Dallas, Texas, the flash... apparently official... President Kennedy died at 1 p.m. central standard time, some thirty-eight minutes ago." Cronkite held back his tears.

It is said that most people can remember exactly where they were the moment they heard this news. Almost sixty years on, there are still many who refuse to accept the official version of exactly who was behind it.

JFK

It was warm, sunny, and bright in Dallas the day the president came to visit; a reflection of a country basking in the hope of a new decade. By 1963, the United States and its young, charming, and handsome Commander-in-Chief were brimming with vibrant optimism. During almost three years in office, Kennedy had faced down the Russians in the Cuban Missile Crisis, was supporting civil rights, and had kick-started a space program that would see "a new generation" of Americans land on the Moon.

Even in the usually conservative state of Texas, Kennedy and his wife Jackie caused a storm of excitement and having greeted the hordes of people at the airport with handshakes, the couple set off in an open-top motorcade to receive more adulation from the thousands lining the streets. As his Lincoln Continental turned into Dealey Plaza, Nellie Connally, the wife of the state governor John Connally, turned to Kennedy and said, "Mr. President, you can't say Dallas doesn't love you." Moments later, having passed the Texas School Book Depository, shots were fired. The president was hit twice, once in the neck, and once in the head. The car rushed to the nearby Parkland Memorial Hospital, where he was declared dead.

Just moments before his assassination, President Kennedy and his wife, Jackie, greeted their adoring Dallas public.

The now infamous grassy knoll, where it is thought a second assassin fired shots at the president.

Two days later, at the same hospital, another man died. His name was Lee Harvey Oswald. An employee at the book depository, and a man known to have links to Soviet Russia, Oswald had been arrested immediately after the shooting. He had stated that he was merely a "patsy" because he had lived in Russia, but for forty-eight hours Oswald was deemed to be the "lone wolf" who had destroyed a country. On the morning of November 24, a local bar owner called Jack Ruby shot Oswald at point blank range while he was being escorted to an armored car by police officials. The shooting was aired live on television. Suddenly, the world's suspicions were aroused.

WHO KILLED JFK?

It's a question that may never be answered. Many have tried. Many theories have been bizarre (author Milton Cooper was sure aliens had had Kennedy killed because he was about to expose Washington-alien collusion), some close to home (many point to Texan oil barons who were fervently anti-Kennedy because of new taxations his regime had brought against the oil industry).

However, most have centered around the fact that the Warren Commission (the inquiry into the assassination) decreed that Oswald and then Ruby had acted alone, and that was that. Surely, that was too easy? Oliver Stone, who made the 1991 movie *JFK*, argued that it was pure "naivety" for the American people to believe it.

In 1975, with the United States and its politics gripped by post-Watergate suspicion, a late-night chat show called *Good Night America* showed a home movie of the assassination called the Zapruder film, named for the man who filmed it. Also used as important evidence by the Warren Commission, the film graphically captures the shot to Kennedy's head, and while it shocked viewers, the point of impact strongly suggested that this must have come from another gun. In 1976, a new Select Committee on Assassinations was set up, and although it found no evidence of overseas or CIA involvement, it did conclude that a second gunman, probably stationed above a grassy knoll alongside the road, had been jointly responsible.

Suddenly there was contradiction, and with that came allegations. Famously there was a man photographed holding an umbrella despite the sunshine, and thought to have been sending signals to potential accomplices.

Live in front of television cameras just two days after Kennedy's death, the suspected assassin, Lee Harvey Oswald, was shot dead by local bar owner Jack Ruby.

"Umbrella Man," as he became known, was even accused of firing a poisonous dart from his umbrella.

Far-fetched perhaps, but what was clear was that the Warren Commission and certain agencies were quick to blame only Oswald. He had communist beliefs as a motive, and when J. Edgar Hoover, the head of the FBI, wrote a memo saying, "The thing I am most concerned about is having something issued so we can convince the public that Oswald is the real assassin," it was clear that an agenda was set.

It was argued that Oswald had visited Mexico prior to the shooting, a trip that indicated possible links to both Fidel Castro's regime in Cuba, and Soviet officials who some argued might have used him to kill Kennedy. On top of that, any Soviet involvement would have been covered up by the US Government, as any retaliation would have caused a war that would have killed millions in a matter of hours.

Cuba's involvement also emerges when theorists suggest the Mafia were behind the assassination. The Mafia, who had lost huge business interests in Cuba after Castro's revolution, resented Kennedy's failed bid to remove him in 1961. The clear links between the mob and Jack Ruby, ignored by the Warren Commission, plus the attempts by Robert Kennedy (the Attorney General and brother of JFK) to prosecute mobsters, all suggest the involvement of organized crime.

Whoever killed Kennedy, it is widely believed that they were helped by the CIA and other inside factions. On the day of the killing, an English journalist on a local newspaper took a phone call. A voice simply urged the reporter to call the US Embassy for "some big news." It was twenty-five minutes before the shootings took place.

At best, the CIA was said to have known all about Oswald's dealings with Soviet and Cuban officials, but allowed any plot to continue as they wanted Kennedy killed. At worst, it is argued by some that the CIA plotted the assassination on the orders of Vice-President Lyndon B. Johnson as part of a coup d'état, due to Kennedy's strong resistance to sending further US troops to Vietnam.

Members of the
Warren Commission,
who unconvincingly
found that Oswald
and Ruby had
acted alone.

THE SKEPTICS

It is estimated that 42 groups, 82 assassins, and 214 other individuals have been named in association with the assassination of President Kennedy, and in US polls as many as 70 percent of people remain sure that this was a broader plot than merely Oswald acting as a lone wolf.

But there remain voices of doubt. Both the Warren Commission and the Select Committee on Assassinations found no evidence of Cuban, Soviet, or CIA involvement (Castro himself argued that he would have been a fool to plan the assassination as his country would have been annihilated), and recent high-tech recreations using state-of-the-art computer simulations suggest the shots came solely from the book depository.

And then there is the sheer size of the cover up. In 1966, renowned US political journalist Roscoe Drummond wrote, "If there were a conspiracy to cover up the truth about the assassination, it would have to involve the Chief Justice, the Republican, Democratic, and non-party members of the commission, the FBI, the CIA, the Secret Service, the distinguished doctors of the armed services— and the White House—a conspiracy so multiple and complex that it would have fallen of its own weight."

THE
DEATH OF
DR. DAVID KELLY

THE CONSPIRACY: ....DR. DAVID KELLY DID
                          NOT COMMIT SUICIDE

LOCATION: ....OXFORDSHIRE, ENGLAND

DATE: .... JULY 17, 2003

Dr. David Kelly was an important man, but he wasn't famous. At least
not until May 2003, when suddenly his name hit the headlines and
he was forced into the limelight around the world. Journalists had
named Kelly as their source for a news report claiming the British
government's dossier on Iraq's weapon capability had been exaggerated
in order to justify an invasion. The story created a media storm, with
David Kelly at the center of it.

Kelly became the subject of mass interest from the media and
politicians alike, and then, having disappeared from his home after
going out for a walk, he was found dead in a nearby wood. On the
surface, it looked like a tragic but simple suicide... but for many
observers, this was surely something more sinister.

KELLY'S CAREER AND DEATH

In May 2003, not long after US and British troops had gone into Iraq, David Kelly met Andrew Gilligan, the Defence and Diplomatic Correspondent for BBC Radio 4's *Today* program. Kelly was a leading expert in microbiology, heading up a division at the Ministry of Defence and working for the United Nations in their examination of Iraq's suspected buildup of weapons of mass destruction (WMDs).

In 2002, the American President, George W. Bush, had named Iraq as part of an "axis of evil." The British government published a dossier stating that Iraq was producing chemical and biological weapons that could be used against foreign foes as well as its own people. They claimed that these could be deployed in just forty-five minutes following the order to use them. Kelly had been privy to the report, even making notes on it, and so, in a London hotel, he and Gilligan spoke off the record for thirty minutes. On May 29, Gilligan was on air reporting that senior officials had told him that the government felt the original copy was "bland," that it needed to be "sexed up," later saying that the forty-five minutes claim had been added to do just that.

The BBC journalist Andrew Gilligan reported that the government's dossier on Iraq's weapons of mass destruction had been "sexed up."

The fallout was explosive; relations between the BBC and the government were worse than tense, and in time Kelly's name, despite Gilligan meeting several other officials, was put forward as his source, placing Kelly at the forefront of what had become potentially a devastating embarrassment for Tony Blair.

Despite not recognizing the words as anything he might have said, Kelly was called to appear in front of the Intelligence and Security, and Foreign Affairs Select Committees. The fact that the latter would be televised upset Kelly, who was uncomfortable with the limelight now upon him, but nevertheless under intense scrutiny, Kelly calmly stated that he remained sure he would not have made the claims reported and that he was not in some way "a fall guy," going on to say the government's dossier was "an accurate document, I think it is a fair reflection of the intelligence that was available and it's presented in a very sober and factual way."

The following day, July 17, Kelly went for a walk near his Oxfordshire home, but didn't return. Police and a volunteer search party were deployed to look for him; the next morning they found his body in a nearby wood. Kelly had taken twenty-nine painkillers and cut the artery on his left wrist.

Dr. Kelly was found dead in these small woods near his Oxfordshire home.

Prime Minister Tony Blair
(left) and President George
W. Bush preparing to take
on the "axis of evil."

A GOVERNMENT UNDER SCRUTINY

Three days later, at a Downing Street press conference, the BBC's Andrew Marr asked the question most were thinking. "Did you assassinate him?" It was batted away, but it was clear the press and the public were suspicious.

Blair ordered a public inquiry, led by Lord Hutton, who in 2004 said, "I am satisfied that Dr. Kelly took his own life by cutting his left wrist and that his death was hastened by his taking Co-proxamol tablets. I am further satisfied that there was no involvement by a third person in Dr. Kelly's death."

But the very fact that an inquiry was called for, along with a raft of other curious evidence, meant that Kelly's death remained hugely controversial. Blair had called for the inquiry within two hours of Kelly's body being found, even before formal identification had taken place. Also, by calling for the inquiry, there could by law be no coroner's inquest. It was as if someone in the government knew the body was there prior to 9.20 a.m., when the search party found it.

There were no prints found on the knife given as evidence although Kelly was not wearing gloves. Mai Pederson, a friend of Kelly's who worked in Iraq with him, argued that there was no way Kelly could use his right hand to make such a cut as he had an old injury that meant he "had difficulty cutting a steak," before also pointing out that Kelly had recently found Bahá'í faith, a religion that forbids suicide. Pederson was never asked to give evidence to Lord Hutton.

The paramedics who attended were confused by the lack of blood at the scene, and the police officers in charge were also never asked to testify. One policeman noted that the scene seemed "extraordinarily contrived" and all had noted that the body was still warm when they found it, although helicopters searching for Kelly equipped with thermo-imaging equipment flew directly over the woods but detected nothing.

At the Hutton Inquiry, much was made of Kelly's supposed diminishing mental health. On July 8, he had hurriedly left for Cornwall with his wife to escape the scrutiny, and it is said he did so in a panic. Mrs. Kelly told the inquiry that they stopped for the night in Weston-Super-Mare in Somerset, on the west coast of England, although witnesses said Kelly was in fact playing cribbage (a card game) in a pub near his Oxfordshire home that night, and that he "seemed fine." No one in that pub was asked to appear in front of Hutton.

Suspicions centered on the government themselves but in 2007, *The Strange Death of David Kelly* was published by UK politician Norman Baker, arguing that Kelly had been murdered in revenge by Iraqi supporters of Saddam Hussein. Baker suggested that the Thames Valley police had covered it up as a suicide, as the government feared further political consequences.

That same year, a BBC poll found that 22.7 percent of respondents believed that Kelly had not killed himself, and while much has been written about the questions that remain unanswered, in 2010 it was disclosed that Lord Hutton had requested that all files relating to the autopsy be kept secret for seventy years, not to conceal evidence but to save Kelly's family any further distress. However, there are still calls for a full inquest into Kelly's death.

The death of
Dr. Kelly remains
one of the most
suspicious events
of modern times.

THE SKEPTICS

Plenty of people have used Kelly's death as a stick to beat Tony Blair's government with, but many argue that while the British government may be guilty of underhand behavior over the years, the notion that they would have murdered a British citizen, especially one so prominently in the spotlight the day after he gave evidence, is too far-fetched.

It was also clear that Kelly was very good at his job, but that he had become a pawn in a battle between the British government and the intelligence services over the conflicting claims regarding Iraq's WMDs. Such was the political fallout and the scrutiny put upon him, it is thought that Kelly could take no more, and ended it quickly on that summer's day in an Oxfordshire wood.

THE DISAPPEARANCE OF HAROLD HOLT

THE CONSPIRACY: ....THE AUSTRALIAN PRIME
MINISTER'S DEATH WAS NO ACCIDENT

LOCATION: ....VICTORIA, AUSTRALIA

DATE: .... DECEMBER 17, 1967

It had been a hot Sunday morning in the Australian state of Victoria. The country's prime minister, Harold Holt, had been driving with friends, and was heading home for a barbecue lunch. To work up an appetite, he suggested a swim at a local beach and was never seen again. Police and coastguards scoured the ocean and the coast for days, searching for the missing politician—presumed to have drowned—but they could find nothing. Five days after his disappearance, a memorial service was held for Harold Holt. Half a century later, talk of conspiracy still lingers on.

THE BACKGROUND

Harold Holt was a career politician. Having entered politics at the tender age of twenty-seven, he became a government minister at thirty, and in January 1966, at fifty-seven, Australia's prime minister. Holt was a fiercely independent man, who refused security detail, saying that it would alienate him from the general public, but such gallant thoughts had to change just months into his leadership when a window in his office was shattered by a sniper's bullet. Soon after, the leader of the opposition survived an attempt on his life. Things would change. Holt had been a firm supporter of US involvement in the Vietnam War and had promised an unpopular escalation in Australian numbers being sent there. An officer was assigned but Holt refused to have any protection during his vacations.

Just a week before Christmas in 1967, Holt went on a trip. A keen outdoorsman, he planned to scuba dive, snorkel, and do some spearfishing with friends. Holt was always in the sea, so much so his doctor had advised that he cut down. His press officer, Tony Eggleton, followed suit. "Look Tony, what are the odds of a prime minister being drowned or taken by a shark?" Holt said.

That Sunday, Holt went swimming on a beach he knew well. Of his four companions, only one joined him in the water, as they felt the conditions were dangerous and that the clear rip tides and known undercurrents would

Prime Minister Holt had pledged more Australian troops to the Vietnam War prior to his disappearance.

be too strong for them. Holt though went out beyond the surf and took on the large swells, before disappearing from view. There was no panic, no call for help; he simply vanished.

THE BODY WAS NEVER FOUND

Without physical evidence of Harold Holt's death, those disputing the official line that he simply drowned have been vocal with their thoughts and theories.

This was the height of the Cold War and the conflict in Vietnam was raging, so suspicions gravitated toward the involvement of a foreign enemy. One example of the many theories that were emerging comes in a letter written at the time from a US lawyer to an Australian colleague, stating, "My hunch from fragmentary press reports is there's a better-than 50 percent chance that Mr. Holt's death was not accidental, but resulted from expert sabotage, probably foreign." Apart from the communist threat, there have been plenty of other theories. Holt was drugged that morning, an assassination. Holt had taken his own life. Holt was part of a crime syndicate and murdered.

What became clear is the people that Holt spent his last morning with included his mistress, Marjorie Gillespie, her daughter, and two family friends of hers. Holt's wife had previously claimed that his aversion to security guards while he was on vacation was on account of his affairs, and so there are those who believe that Holt actually faked his death to be with Ms. Gillespie and remained in hiding for the rest of his life.

However, it is the backdrop of the Cold War that has most fueled suggestions about what really happened to Holt. A known friend of US President Lyndon B. Johnson, was Holt kidnapped by a submarine and taken to Communist China to be interrogated for inside political secrets?

A more outlandish suggestion came in 1983, when a book called *The Prime Minister was a Spy* was published. Its author, Anthony Grey, claimed that Holt was in fact a Communist spy and that day was "saved" by the Chinese. The story is that Holt knowingly swam out beyond the surf, that he was given equipment and taken beneath the waves by scuba divers, swam to a submarine waiting offshore, and was taken away for a new life in China.

Cheviot Beach
in Victoria, where
Holt went for
his (supposedly)
last swim.

THE SKEPTICS

Holt's family members and colleagues understand that due to them never finding his body, speculation is to be expected. Tony Eggleton later said, "Basically I think that people just find it very hard to accept that a prime minister can go for a swim on a Sunday afternoon, like anyone else, and end up misjudging the situation and drowning. But that's what happened on that afternoon forty years ago."

The notion that there was a submarine waiting to either kidnap the prime minister or save him is also debunked. Robert Holt, his grandson, points out that the beach is too shallow, and that the currents are too strong in the area to harbor a submarine. Holt's widow Zara scoffed at the idea that Holt lived out his life in China, saying, "Harold didn't like Chinese food."

THE ILLUMINATI

THE CONSPIRACY: ......A POWERFUL GROUP MADE
UP OF POLITICIANS AND INFLUENCERS
CONTROLS THE WORLD

LOCATION: .... WORLDWIDE

DATE: .... 1776-PRESENT DAY

In 2011, Beyoncé asked in a song "Who runs the world?" Her answer
was "Girls," but there are many people who believe that the world is in
fact run by a secret society known as the Illuminati, a group in which
she herself and her husband Jay-Z, along with swathes of other
powerful celebrities and politicians, are prominent members.

It is said that the Illuminati work in the shadows, using their members'
considerable influence to control global events, manipulating
everything from wars to elections. They take their strength not only
from the corridors of political power but also from the vast domains
of entertainment and the media. Their domination knows no bounds.

In 1776, a group known as the Illuminati was founded in Bavaria by a former Jesuit and professor of Law called Adam Weishaupt. Interested in the Freemasons but put off by their fees, Weishaupt's aim was to replace Christianity with "a religion of reason." Membership grew quickly, thoughts were shared, obedience was pledged, and influence grew. Anyone over thirty wasn't to be trusted, as their religious thoughts were seen as archaic. However, their influence was growing so rapidly that in 1785, a new law was passed in Bavaria banning all such secret societies, and so the Illuminati disappeared...

THE MODERN ILLUMINATI

... Or so it was thought. Rumors had persisted after their disbandment that they had influenced the Battle of Waterloo and that it was they who were behind the French Revolution. Those whispers didn't become anything louder until the 1970s. First published in 1975, the three novels collectively titled *The Illuminati Trilogy* shed light on this supposedly still active group, which was becoming more powerful and increasingly influential. Rumors spread rapidly but with the onset of the Internet in the mid-1990s, these rumors turned to serious speculation. Was there really a secret society influencing every major event on Earth?

An early initiation into the original Illuminati in the eighteenth century.

The 1963 assassination of President Kennedy, NASA's Moon landings, 9/11, political elections, the rise and falls of global stock markets, wars, pandemics; all have been organized and influenced by the group who secretly oversee this New World Order, where a gang of authoritarian elitists exist to cause the eventual end of nation states.

MEMBERS AND THEIR SYMBOLS

It is said that President Thomas Jefferson was an early member, setting the tone for political influencers, but while those with political power are either involved or handpicked by the Illuminati, there are growing suspicions that the world of celebrity has been infiltrated and wields more and more control within the secret society's impenetrable walls.

Madonna's 2015 single "Illuminati" was perhaps a too obvious clue to her apparent involvement in the group, but she did once tell an interviewer that she knew who the members were. It has been suggested that she is joined by Kim Kardashian and her ex-husband Kanye West, and that Lady Gaga, Rhianna, and Katy Perry join them from the world of pop. Perry once said in an interview, "I guess you've kind of made it when they think you're in the Illuminati."

Perhaps the most prominent public figures rumored to be involved with the Illuminati are Beyoncé and Jay-Z, both being instrumental in pushing the group's agenda through their music. Beyoncé's 2013 Super Bowl performance was maligned by the likes of right-wing pundit and renowned conspiracy theorist Mark Dice, who said her performances were full of "elaborate Illuminati rituals hidden in plain sight," going on to call both she and Jay-Z "Illuminati puppets" and "Satanic skanks." Jay-Z, on stage and in pictures, has often used a hand signal that depicts a triangle. Officially, it is a diamond, a jewel synonymous with his record label and his wife has also made the gesture in support, but many are quick to point out that it is a symbol long connected with the Illuminati.

"The Eye of Providence," an eye enclosed in a triangle or a pyramid, has been associated with Freemason groups since the late eighteenth century, and the fact that it is now found on the US$1 bill strengthens beliefs that the Illuminati today remain influential and are growing in power.

The "Eye of Providence" on the US dollar bill and a possible clue to the existence of the modern Illuminati.

THE SKEPTICS

The presence of "The Eye of Providence" on the dollar bill might seem like a clue to the Illuminati's existence from Dan Brown's 2000 novel *Angels and Demons*, but instead it represents divine providence, and the idea that God watches over humanity. Furthermore, Robert Wilson, a coauthor of *The Illuminati Trilogy* distanced himself from any suggestion of the idea that the group exists, claiming that the books were simply part of a counterculture hoax including fake letters being sent to *Playboy* magazine, alluding to a secret society that had been behind various major events including the assassination of JFK.

It is, however, a theory that won't go away. As recently as 2016, the year Donald Trump came to office in the United States, a poll was taken in which 15 percent of (mainly Republican) voters believed in it. "An estimated 200 million Americans were registered to vote in the 2016 presidential election," said the poll's website. "If [it] is an accurate picture of the entire US population, 30 million of those voters would be people who believe in the Illuminati."

REPTILIAN
OVERLORDS

THE CONSPIRACY: ....THE WORLD IS RUN BY LIZARDS FROM OUTER-SPACE

LOCATION: .... WORLDWIDE

DATE: ....100,000 BC-PRESENT DAY

They are among us, but you won't see them. They can look like us, but they aren't human. And they are ruling our world but we don't know it. Not all of us anyway. Some know the truth, they know that reptilian overlords from outer-space, able to shape-shift and take on human forms, are in control of our royal families, our political hierarchies, and they are manipulating everything we love and hold dear.

They are flesh-eating, they are blood drinking, and they are your leaders, they are your favorite singer, your favorite actor, and since the dawn of time, they have been responsible for all the wrongdoings on Earth.

Images of reptilian humanoids have appeared in science fiction literature for many decades. Robert E. Howard, the author of *Conan The Barbarian*, used the serpent people as his evil protagonists in works such as "The Shadow Kingdom," a short story first published in 1929. The dangerous creatures with human bodies and snake-like heads continued to appear in fantasy literature, but when in 1999 *The Biggest Secret*, a book by former British sports reporter David Icke was published, the reptilian race stepped from fiction into a terrifying reality.

CREATURE FROM THE BLACK LAGOON

starring
RICHARD CARLSON · JULIA ADAMS

with
RICHARD DENNING · ANTONIO MORENO
NESTOR PAIVA · WHIT BISSELL

Life can be stranger than fiction! A poster for the 1954 movie *Creature from the Black Lagoon*—but what if these creatures really do walk among us?

DAVID ICKE

Icke had already become known as something of a British eccentric when he appeared on television chat shows, stating he was the son of God, and for a while only being seen wearing turquoise. He had become an advocate of model realism, a school of thought that all possible worlds are real and that they exist and are no different from the world we know. That brought him to his theory about a reptilian race.

A believer in New Age philosophies and reincarnation, Icke argues that the reptilian race stems from the star Alpha Draconis in the Draco constellation; a constellation shaped like a dragon. They first formed there in ancient times, but started to infiltrate humanity around 300,000 years ago, and were probably responsible for the creation of Adam.

Since then they have hijacked the world, living in underground bases, mating with humans, but also able to modify the perception of any human being so that we see what they want us to see, therefore hiding their actual seven-foot tall reptilian appearances.

In an interview Icke said, "When you get back into the ancient world, you find this recurring theme of a union between a non-human race and humans—creating a hybrid race. From 1998, I started coming across people who told me they had seen people change into a non-human form. It's an age-old phenomenon known as shape-shifting. The basic form is like a scaly humanoid, with reptilian rather than humanoid eyes."

WHO ARE THEY?

The theory is that from ancient times, the world's leaders have been related to these reptilian overlords and have the power to control the events that shape the world and impact on humanity. It is suggested that those involved include Sumerian leaders, Egyptian pharaohs, the Rothschild family, the Rockefellers, and royal bloodlines all over the world including the British (Queen Elizabeth II is said to be one and Icke said the Queen Mother was "seriously reptilian"). In American politics suspects include the Bush family, Barack Obama, Donald Trump, and in keeping with other conspiracy theories, it is argued that these reptilians are responsible for groups such as the Freemasons, the Illuminati, and their New World Order.

And don't think it's just those in power. It has been suggested that entertainers dating back to Bob Hope, more modern singers such as Katie Perry and Rhianna, and actors such as Angelina Jolie are all part of the conspiracy. A US poll in 2013 indicated that 4 percent of the country's registered voters believed that lizard people control politics.

David Icke once told an interviewer that the former British Prime Minister Ted Heath had eyes that could turn jet black, a sign of his links to the reptilian clan. Those who believe Icke's theories and follow him closely have other suggestions of what to look for. Reddish hair, a low pulse, a love of outer-space, piercing eyes, and unexplained scars are just a few of the signs.

The British eccentric, David Icke, has long campaigned that the world is run by reptiles.

THE SKEPTICS

While often laughed off, more serious accusations have been aimed at Icke and his theory. Some conclude that he is in fact anti-Semitic, a claim he refutes. Others look at his website, his books, and his talks all over the world that attract large numbers and say that this is merely a publicity stunt. His books sold 140,000 copies between 1998 and 2011, making him around $2,800,000; they have been translated into eleven languages. By 2006 his website was getting 600,000 hits a week. His lectures have seen him talk in twenty-five countries. In 2008 he spoke for seven hours to 2,500 people in London and he generated nearly $120,000 in ticket sales when he spoke in Melbourne, Australia in 2010.

His popularity and the widespread support for his theory prove that there is a huge appetite for what he has to say, and if Icke is right and we are being ruled by reptiles, they might just have met their match.

THE
DEATH OF
PABLO ESCOBAR

THE CONSPIRACY: ......EVENTS LEADING TO THE
DRUG-LORD'S SHOOTING REMAIN UNCLEAR

LOCATION: ....MEDELLÍN, COLOMBIA

DATE: .... DECEMBER 2, 1993

Eight men pose for the camera. They squat over their dead prey. Powerful rifles in hand, five of them are in official uniform, and they smile. They are victorious. The photograph resembles a group of big game hunters, congratulating themselves after bringing down a dangerous wild animal.

But this is the body of a man. Pablo Escobar, the most notorious, the most wanted, and certainly the richest criminal the world has ever known. Shot dead as he tried to escape his pursuers, fleeing across the tiled rooftop near his hideout in an otherwise unremarkable, middle-class *barrio* (neighborhood) in the Colombian city of Medellín. His T-shirt rides up, showing off a wealthy stomach, his face is covered in blood; a gunshot to the side of the head, the final act in an extraordinary life.

Individuals and organizations in equal measure have both taken credit and distanced themselves from Escobar's death, but who was actually behind the killing?

THE VILLAIN OR THE HERO?

Known as "*El Patron*" or The Boss, Escobar was the head of the Medellín Cartel, a drug-smuggling corporation that amassed an estimated fortune of over $30 billion by monopolizing the cocaine trade into the United States in the late 1970s, 1980s, and early 1990s.

Having founded his cartel in the mid-1970s, it is said that he was soon overseeing monthly shipments of up to eighty tons of the drug into the country, but building vast power and wealth came at a huge cost to human life. Members of potential rival cartels (in both Colombia and abroad), police officials, politicians, the judiciary, innocent locals, addicts; all were under his power and many became victims in the drug war that earned his country the title "the murder capital of the world."

In 1982, with his empire growing, Pablo Escobar stepped into politics. It was a move that unsettled many in his country but as an alternative member of Colombia's Chamber of Representatives, he was able to make many social changes, funding huge construction projects in social housing and sporting venues built for the poor, and making him a hero of the people.

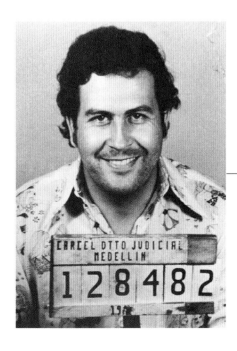

Escobar was arrested in 1977 for a minor crime, but his cheeky smile suggests he knew he had bigger fish to fry.

By 1992, Escobar was on the run. A year earlier he had surrendered to the authorities, and was sentenced to five years in jail, but Escobar had struck a deal with Colombia's President César Gaviria that enabled him to serve his time in a comfortable penitentiary he had built himself called La Catedral. In time though, those same authorities attempted to move him to a conventional correctional facility and so he escaped, sparking a national manhunt.

WHO KILLED HIM?

The day after his forty-fourth birthday, Pablo Escobar was finally killed. But who was responsible? The official line is that Escobar was killed by a special government unit, set up specifically to seek him out. However, there are still many who dispute that, from rival cartels to close family members.

In 1986, the Colombian president had created Search Bloc, a special operations unit of the National Police of Colombia; its sole purpose was to

A photograph taken during the raid by Colombian forces on December 2, 1993, that led to Escobar's death.

apprehend Escobar and his associates. Trained by the Colombian military, its members selected to be impervious to the usual high levels of police corruption, the group was assisted by US intelligence, US special forces, and the CIA (the US Government, under President Ronald Reagan, had waged a "war on drugs"). For years, they had met strong resistance from Escobar's cartel, with bloody battles continuing to define the country.

The day before his death, Escobar had quietly celebrated with a cake, wine, and some marijuana, apparently completely unaware that those seeking him out were moving ever closer. Using the most up-to-date technology to track Escobar's cellphone transmissions, the Search Bloc's group of eight men entered the house in which he was hiding out by blowing down the door, engaged in a gun fight with Escobar and his bodyguard, before killing them both as they fled across the neighboring roof. Escobar was killed with a single shot in the side of the head. "Viva, Colombia!" the men were said to have shouted.

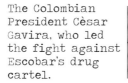

The Colombian President Cèsar Gavira, who led the fight against Escobar's drug cartel.

However, there are differing accounts. Credit for the killing is also claimed by Los Pepes, formed in January 1993 and made up of rival drug traffickers, paramilitaries, and former members of Escobar's own cartel, now scorned and extremely vengeful. Wanting Escobar dead, it is said that with the help of the CIA and the Colombian National Police, they set out to catch and kill the drug-lord, and in the last months of his life, Escobar was at war with them. Many accounts say there were Los Pepes members with Search Bloc that day, and it was in fact a central figure within their group who fired his M16 and killed El Patron. Others are convinced that the CIA and US military not only sanctioned the killing, but that one of their men actually pulled the trigger.

While those who wanted him dead celebrated his final downfall, Escobar's loved ones have a further theory that it was actually suicide. "I have no doubt," said Sebastián Marroquín, Escobar's son (he adopted a new name) in an interview in 2014.

Marroquín went on to say that his father on numerous occasions told him that should anyone ever have him cornered, he would shoot himself in his right ear rather than be captured alive. In the photo of the armed men posing over his dead body, Escobar's Sig Sauer pistol is lying next to him, further fueling the family theory that he shot himself. The family also believe that Escobar knew very well that those charged with finding him had the best in telecommunication technology, but he stayed on the phone to both his son and a radio show that day, hoping to be caught, wanting to put an end to the fighting.

Pablo Escobar
remains a
divisive figure
in Colombia
and beyond.

THE SKEPTICS

It seems that even in death, Pablo Escobar divides opinions and emotions. Twenty-five thousand people turned up at his funeral, mourning his demise. Others celebrated the end of a bloody era. With such division, claims and accusations came from various sources, helping to obscure the truth.

Diego Fernando Murillo, aka Don Berna, was a leading member of the Los Pepes group. He has since said that his members were indeed there that day, and that it was his own brother, Rodolfo Murillo, who shot Escobar. His evidence was backed up by a 2003 confession from a former paramilitary member who admitted it had been a joint operation. Fidel Castaño, another paramilitary and cofounder of Los Pepes, refutes the claim, denying that his group ever performed an operation with the Secret Bloc. "The operation during which Escobar was killed was realized exclusively by the police, as is public knowledge," he said.

US involvement, specifically CIA, has not been disproven and suspicions remain. Recently, federal judges in Washington have ruled that they need to release documentation on what happened that day—documentation that has long been withheld despite the Freedom of Information Act.

As for the family claims of suicide, Colonel Hugo Martinez, the Search Bloc leader, categorically denies them, stating that any gunshot from within three feet would have left gunpowder marks on Escobar's face. According to his statement and that of other witnesses, there were no such marks visible in the autopsy photos.

THE
BILDERBERG
MEETINGS

THE CONSPIRACY: .... A POWERFUL AND
     ENIGMATIC GROUP IS PREPARING
       FOR GLOBAL DOMINATION

LOCATION: .... EUROPE AND UNITED STATES

DATE .... 1954-PRESENT DAY

What happens at the Bilderberg meetings and should the world be
concerned about what has over the years become an enigmatic and
secretive group? Set up in 1954, and taking its name from the
Bilderberg Hotel in the Netherlands where the inaugural meeting took
place, the group invites leading figures from finance, business, politics,
academia, and the media from the United States and Europe to discuss
and "bolster a consensus around free-market Western capitalism and
its interests around the world."

However, the secrecy that surrounds the group and the meetings has
invited suspicion, and after half a century that secrecy is still very
much in evidence. This has led many to believe that behind their
permanently closed doors, the Bilderberg group is plotting a New
World Order and preparing for global domination.

Nearly ten years after the end of the Second World War, and the various crises that threatened the world were no less worrying. The Soviet Union's dominance of Eastern Europe was leading to an increase in anti-US sentiment that was leaking into western parts of the continent. It was under that cloud that several politicians and luminaries sought to create a line of communication that would promote "Atlanticism" and a better understanding between the two cultures, preventing further chances of war and fostering cooperation both politically and economically.

SUSPICIONS GROW

By the mid-1960s, speculation was mounting about what was actually being decided behind the Bilderberg group's closed doors. With the backdrop of the Cold War, and with the world's superpowers deemed to be increasingly hell-bent on global control, those on the right and the left began to take a closer look (or as close as they could). They decided that this powerful newly

Powerful figures such as Bill Gates (left) and former President Bill Clinton continue to attend the Bilderberg group's meetings.

formed group was coming together to make decisions about how to further enslave the world.

The official line is that these are merely informal discussions, a place for US and European figureheads to meet and thrash out the problems facing the global population, both rich and poor. Cyber security, Iran, Russia, election rigging—all may be deliberated upon and because no minutes are ever taken of the meetings, and no statements made, no political party lines ever need be met. Executives from multinational companies including Google, Shell Oil, and BP have been joined by high-profile global figures such as Margaret Thatcher, Bill Clinton, Bill Gates, Helmut Kohl, José Manuel Barroso, and Prince Charles to explore solutions to the world's ills, but critics wonder what these elitist attendees (mostly male) actually know and understand about the problems they proclaim to want to eradicate.

Over the years, these are the individuals, the power-brokers, and the companies that have most benefited from transatlantic postwar capitalism, so those who doubt their motives argue that there is no motivation to make any real changes, and that if they are merely discussing the public's problems, what is the point? "Your fillet steak always tastes better if it has been accompanied by a small side-helping of self-congratulation," wrote one observer. Protesters picket the gates at every meeting, disturbed by what they see as much more than a discussion group and possibly a shadowy "world government." Both sides of the political spectrum distrust the organization. On the left, there is a theory that the group plans to uphold and impose further capitalist domination, while those on the right argue that they are plotting to impose a world government and a planned economy.

Many believe that the Republican Party in the United States had been infiltrated by elitist intellectuals dominated by members of Bilderberg, and their internationalist policies would lead to global communism. In 2006, a book called *The Secrets of the Bilderberg Club* by Daniel Estulin describes "sinister cliques and the Bilderberg lobbyists" manipulating the public "to install a world government that knows no borders and is not accountable to anyone but its own self."

Former British Chancellor of the Exchequer Denis Healey was a founder of the Bilderberg group and advocated some sort of "one-world government."

THE SKEPTICS

Despite the clandestine nature of the Bilderberg group and their meetings, there are those directly involved who have long been prepared to discuss its motives. In 2001, Denis Healey, a Bilderberg group founder and a committee member for over thirty years, gave an interview and answered the critics. "To say we are striving for one-world government is exaggerated, but not wholly unfair," he admitted. "Those of us in Bilderberg felt we couldn't go on forever fighting one another for nothing and killing people and rendering millions homeless. So we felt that a single community throughout the world would be a good thing."

Plenty of others see the meetings as merely a distasteful annual seminar where the world's rich and powerful meet, eat the finest foods, and drink the finest wines, but nothing of any note really takes place. "If the participants at Bilderberg really want to explore global challenges, talking to each other is the last thing that they should be doing," wrote one observer. "We already know that the powerful organize the world for us—it is common knowledge. What Bilderberg exposes is that what goes on at endless summits and conferences across the globe is a mountain of smugness that is much more frightening than anoraks muttering about the Illuminati."

THE FLAT

EARTH

THE CONSPIRACY: ......THE EARTH IS FLAT AND
GOVERNMENT AGENCIES ARE
COVERING IT UP

LOCATION: .... WORLDWIDE

DATE: ....THE 1800S-PRESENT DAY

The idea that the planet on which we all live is in reality not spherical but flat can be considered the "godfather of conspiracy theories." For centuries the world's deepest thinkers, its bravest explorers, and the most enlightened philosophers pondered on the shape of the Earth.

The prevalence of scientific thought and methods has given almost universal credence to the belief that the Earth is, like all the planets in our solar system, spherical. However, despite overwhelming scientific and photographic evidence, there is a growing number of individuals and organizations (the Flat Earth Society has significantly increased in size this century) who firmly advocate that our planet is far from spherical, and that those who have taught us otherwise are part of an elaborate cover up.

THE BACKGROUND

Look back to ancient cultures, and you will find beliefs that the world is flat. From early ancient Greek thinking (both Homer and Hesiod depicted the Earth as a disk-like shape on the shield of Achilles), through to the Bronze and Iron Ages in Europe, the Ottoman Empire, ancient India, and China—all these civilizations and more have imagined that our planet is flat.

The idea that the world was actually spherical appears in later ancient Greek philosophy with the likes of Pythagoras, Plato, and Aristotle providing evidence. The notion that the Earth was spherical began to spread through the centuries, but that is not to say it became universally accepted. Take China for example. As late as 1595, a visiting Jesuit missionary noted that scholars in the Ming dynasty believed "The Earth is flat and square, and the

Professor Orlando Ferguson's 1893 map that depicts what he believed to be our "Square and Stationary Earth."

sky is a round canopy." Half a century later, ideas had changed; a Chinese astronomical treatise called "Ge zhi cao" described the world as spherical with "no square corners."

Humanity's wanderlust and desire to explore the planet and beyond has offered actual observational evidence, but could not prevent modern flat Earth beliefs from continuing to grow, especially from the 1800s when large numbers of thinkers rebelled against increasing scientific progress.

FLAT EARTHERS AND THEIR BELIEFS

The fact that when we travel around the Earth it seems to be flat is the simplistic but fundamental evidence behind their theory. They maintain that those who have taught us otherwise are part of a historical "round Earth conspiracy." That is not to say that those who don't believe the Earth is spherical think that it is simply pancake-flat. The theory supported by modern flat Earthers is that we are living on a disk-like shape, with the Arctic Circle at its center, a 150-foot wall of ice around the rim (Antarctica), and underneath there is nothing but rocks.

They explain Earth's day and night cycle by asserting that the Sun and the Moon are of similar size, moving in circles only 3,000 miles above the Earth. Stars, they say, move 3,100 miles above us. They also believe that there is an invisible "antimoon," one that obscures our Moon, explaining any lunar eclipse.

Gravity, as it has been studied and taught, is false, merely an illusion. According to those with flat Earth beliefs, objects do not accelerate toward the ground, but instead the Earth moves upward at thirty-two feet per second, and is driven—not by gravity—but a force they call "dark energy." There is disagreement among them on whether Albert Einstein's theory of relativity is accurate or not, with some arguing that it allows the Earth to accelerate upward without the disk-shaped planet eventually surpassing the speed of light.

Created in 1956, the Flat Earth Society has slowly grown in size, and despite losing numbers in the 1990s today it is growing by 200 new members per year thanks largely to social media and the Internet. YouTube, Facebook,

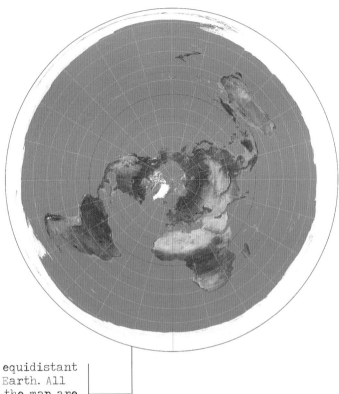

An azimuthal equidistant
projection of Earth. All
the points on the map are
at proportionally correct
distances from the center.

and Twitter have all allowed like-minded theorists to share their beliefs,
despite some criticism from those who maintain that there is no room for
apparent misinformation.

THE CONSPIRACY THEORY

In the latter half of the twentieth century, global governments and most
prominently NASA and the rest of the world's space agencies have pushed
the belief that the Earth is spherical for their own agendas, the most vital
being centered around space travel, or more likely the faking of space travel.
The Flat Earth Society quotes Lyndon Johnson who said in 1958, before he
was president, "Control of space means control of the world." With their

attempts to explore the universe failing, NASA instead faked footage of their space exploration, and by doing so used the long-perceived spherical shape in the images they "gave" the world.

Flat Earthers believe that those photographs have been doctored, pointing to the difference in the color of the oceans and the changing shapes of the continents. They also say that NASA guards stand watch along the Earth's ice wall below the disc, and that pilots are tricked by rigged GPS devices that make them think they are flying in straight lines around a sphere when in fact, they are flying in circles around the disk.

Using the YouTube platform in 2017, one flat Earther flew from Charlotte on the US East Coast to the northwest city of Seattle. Using a spirit level whose bubble did remain centered, he said, "I recorded a twenty-three minute and forty-five second time-lapse, which by those measurements means the plane traveled a little over 203 miles. According to spherical trigonometry given to explain the heliocentric model, this should have resulted in the compensation of five miles of curvature. As you'll see there was no measurable compensation for curvature."

Flat Earthers claim
that NASA has
doctored images of
Earth that showed it
to be spherical.

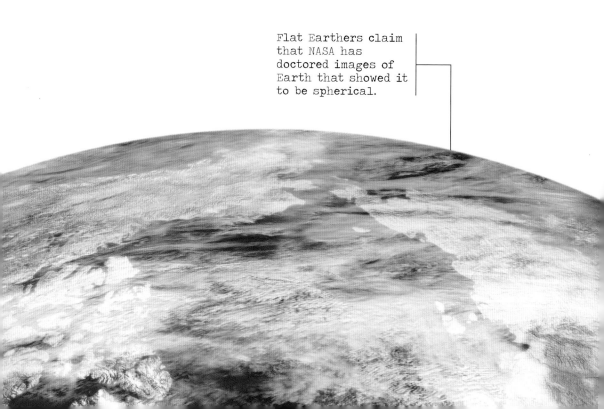

THE SKEPTICS

Modern-day astronomers, scientists, physicists, and explorers (both on our oceans and in space) would without question dismiss the validity of any notion but that of a spherical Earth. Back in the 1400s, Portuguese navigators reported that while traveling around the coast of Africa, they observed that the Sun's position moved farther northward the farther south they traveled, and that its position directly above them at noon showed that they had crossed the equator. The first ever circumnavigation of the planet was a Portuguese expedition led by Ferdinand Magellan in 1512. One of the few survivors, Antonio Pigafetta, recorded the loss of a day in the course of the voyage, thus proving an east–west curvature.

Other arguments against a flat Earth cite the obvious witness accounts from space, but if the conspiracy that NASA and other space agencies have merely fabricated this are true then there are plenty of other natural events that counter the argument. The shape of the Earth's shadow in a partial lunar eclipse is always a near perfect circle; if it was a disk shape, those shapes could only occur at midnight, which they don't. The Earth's seasons vary depending on what hemisphere you are in, due to the Sun's rays striking the planet at different angles, something that could not happen if the Earth's surface was flat.

And then there are the stars. Look up into the sky from a high-latitude location and you will see, among others, the Big and the Little Dippers, but should you then head to the South Pole, none of those same celestial sights will be on show. Instead you will see the Southern Cross, among others. If the Earth were flat, everything in the sky on the night side of the planet would be the same, wherever you were.

3

COVER-UPS

There is a natural explanation
of why humans have always been
fascinated with conspiracy
theories that suggests when it
comes to our most gargantuan
events, we want answers and those
answers must be proportionate to
the event itself. Cover-ups appeal
to this desire for resolution,
and in this chapter we will look
at uncomfortable notions such as
there is a hidden cure for cancer,
that 9/11 was an inside job, and
the Asian tsunami in 2004 was not
a natural disaster.

9/11

THE CONSPIRACY: ..THE ATTACKS ON NEW YORK
AND THE PENTAGON WERE EITHER
KNOWN OF OR PERPETRATED BY
THE US GOVERNMENT

LOCATION: NEW YORK CITY, WASHINGTON DC,
AND PENNSYLVANIA, UNITED STATES

DATE: ....SEPTEMBER 11, 2001

It was just another sunny fall morning in New York. Office blocks were opening, morning coffees and bagels were being consumed, all under a canopy of clear blue that covered the city's iconic skyline. However, up above the hustle and bustle of Manhattan's streets lurked an unknown and unprecedented threat. Passenger jets had been hijacked and were making their way toward the tallest buildings in New York City.

What happened next shocked the world. The Twin Towers of New York's World Trade Center would collapse in less than an hour, and after a number of attacks on the United States that day, almost 3,000 people died. But, even before the dust had settled on a stunned city, people were questioning exactly what they had seen.

MORE THAN A TRAGIC ACCIDENT

Was this just a terrible plane crash? Just before 9 a.m., an American Airlines Boeing 767 (Flight 11) had flown into the North Tower. Smoke billowed from a gaping hole high in the building, as those at street level looked up, aghast at how this terrible accident could have happened.

And then came another plane. Eighteen minutes after the first crash, a United Airlines Boeing 767—Flight 175—arrowed over Manhattan, sharply changed its course and slammed into the South Tower. This was no accident. New York was under attack.

Flames and smoke filled the sky, as did the cries of distress from those witnessing the events from down below, cries that became louder with the news that the Pentagon had also been hit by a plane, before reports that another passenger jet (United Airlines Flight 93) had crashed into a field in Pennsylvania.

The scale of the destruction on September 11, 2001, shocked the entire world.

The destruction at the Pentagon wasn't enough to convince many that it was caused by an airplane.

What was happening? Confusion reigned among the public, but then steel, glass, debris, and dust rained down upon them as the South Tower was followed by the North Tower, both disintegrating, apparently dissolved by the sheer heat of the gallons of burning aviation fuel leaked by the aircraft.

Over 1,000 miles away, President George W. Bush was visiting an elementary school in Florida when a member of his team whispered in his ear to inform him of the attacks. Bush was taken up in the Air Force One jet to plan for what was immediately seen as a terrorist attack. But, on the night of 9/11, whispers began to appear on the Internet. Was everything as clear-cut as it seemed?

"OK, IS IT JUST ME...?"

As the sun set on the United States on September 11, 2001, across the world people were looking to the relatively new Internet for more answers. In the United States itself, one man on an online forum started to discuss with strangers the extraordinary events of the day.

"OK, is it just me," he began, "or did anyone else recognize that it wasn't the airplane impacts that blew up the World Trade Center? To me, this is the most frightening part of this morning. I hope other people actually are catching this, but I haven't seen anyone say it yet, so I guess I will... There's no doubt that the planes hit the building and did a lot of damage. But look at the footage—those buildings were *demolished*."

While stories were published raising various suspicions, firstly in France and then across Europe, in the United States it wasn't until the increasingly unpopular war in Iraq that the public began to question what they had been told. That information had come from the 9/11 Commission, a 585-page report on the attacks, itself becoming a bestseller on its release in 2004. Despite finding that al-Qaeda terrorists had plotted and carried out the attacks, and that the towers had fallen due to the incredible heat caused by the aviation fuel, many weren't convinced. The president and Congress had appointed the representatives on the commission, and so impartiality was questioned. If this was an inside job, the inquiry should have come from outside. Or so said growing numbers of "truthers," as they would be known.

The commission's report did show that the CIA had briefed the president in the summer of 2001 regarding the very real threat from al-Qaeda, but it was thought that the US Government knew the exact details and, with the attacks imminent, the North American Aerospace Defense Command

As leader of al-Qaeda, Osama bin Laden (left) took responsibility for the 9/11 attacks, but was it that straightforward?

(NORAD) issued a stand-down order, deliberately scrambling fighter jets late, allowing the hijacked planes to reach their targets. Many theories have been discussed, ranging from the strange (one suggested that there were no planes at all, but holograms set around US missiles to create an illusion) to the serious, such as Israel's involvement in order to generate global Islamophobia.

The most common theory suggests that the US Government itself orchestrated the attacks, and stems from that early argument that the Twin Towers came down due to explosives, not fuel. A campaign organization called Architects & Engineers for 9/11 Truth argue that steel does not melt until it reaches around 2,800°F (over 1,500°C), open fires of jet fuel—such as those in the Twin Towers inferno—cannot burn hotter than 1,700°F (926°C), and that dust analyzed from the rubble contained microscopic remnants of nano-thermite explosives, which can be tailored for use in controlled demolitions. Eyewitnesses were reported to have heard a number of explosions prior to the towers collapsing.

The falling of a third tower later that afternoon cemented the theory, a building across the street from the Twin Towers, which had not been hit by an airplane. It was struck by large debris and burned for hours, but there was no aviation fuel. Was this the result of controlled explosives too? The third tower was not included in the commission report.

The attacks on the Pentagon and the downing of Flight 93 have also been scrutinized. Conspiracy theorists suggest that Flight 93, officially said to have been downed by passengers and crew rather than surrendering control to the terrorists, was shot down by scrambled jets, a notion supported by the large area covered by its wreckage. Theorists assert that the Pentagon was in fact hit by a US missile or unmanned drone, as the relatively small amount of damage suggests that this was not caused by an airliner.

But why do it? US foreign policy changed considerably after 9/11 and it is argued that the attacks that day were carried out in order to control global oil markets and to justify emerging wars in both Afghanistan and Iraq. It was far from an unprecedented notion, with those making the case citing Operation Northwoods, an unimplemented plan by US Joint Chiefs of Staff in 1962 suggesting that by attacking US cities and blaming these assaults on Fidel Castro's government, the United States could strengthen any case for the invasion of Cuba.

The members of the 9/11 Commission who found that the events of that day constituted a terrorist attack.

THE SKEPTICS

Those who refuse to believe that the US Government could be behind the largest terrorist attack the world has ever seen point to the extensive nature of the 9/11 Commission report and that the "facts" it offers are more than thorough proof of al-Qaeda's guilt. This, they argue, was the first American conspiracy of the digital age, and through the Internet and on modern social media platforms, the theory of US involvement was always going to fester and grow.

The main argument, that the aviation fuel could not have brought down the towers, is questioned by a 2005 report by the National Institute of Standards and Technology who state that the planes sliced through the utility shafts of the buildings, creating the perfect conduit for burning fuel and once combusted, the destruction of both towers was inevitable.

COVID-19

THE CONSPIRACY: .... THE 2020 GLOBAL
PANDEMIC IS A LIE

LOCATION: .... WORLDWIDE

DATE: ..... DECEMBER 31, 2019-PRESENT DAY

On December 31, 2019, government officials in the Chinese city of
Wuhan reported dozens of cases of a pneumonia-like disease, its cause
unknown. Most of the afflicted were vendors or dealers in a local
seafood market, and all were suffering with a fever, difficulty in
breathing, and, in extreme cases, lesions to their lungs.

Just weeks later the disease (now named Covid-19) had spread through
Asia to the Middle East, Europe, Australia, and North and South
America; the reported death toll had grown; and soon the world would
be locked down. But, as fast as Covid spread around the globe, so did
the doubts as to whether it actually existed at all.

Hundreds of people, most with far-right motives, storm Berlin's Reichstag. But this isn't the 1930s, this is August 2020, and their anger is directed at the restrictions imposed due to a pandemic many of them believe is a lie.

Such skepticism regarding Covid-19 is far from restricted to Germany. In many places where the unprecedented restrictions have affected people's freedom, you will find some level of doubt about their legitimacy and anger toward the authorities. The regulations put upon global populations are seen as infringing human rights, the compulsory wearing of masks as the literal muzzling of the people, and the figures (over 3 million deaths up to late April 2021) as having been manipulated to suit a more sinister agenda.

German protestors march on Berlin's Reichstag in August 2020.

THE THEORIES

When the leader of the free world expresses his doubts about a pandemic, it is little wonder that others will follow. On April 3, 2020, the US Centers for Disease Control and Prevention stated that all Americans should wear masks in public. The president at the time, Donald Trump, said, "You don't have to do it. They suggested for a period of time, but this is voluntary. I don't think I'm going to be doing it."

The doubts were fueled. Things were not as they seemed. As early as February 2020, noted conspiracy theorists such as David Icke argued that this was a disease spread due to the roll-out of a new mobile 5G network, prevalent in Wuhan and beyond, but not in use in Africa where cases of Covid-19 were notably low.

Some argued that a meteor landing had caused the disease. Another theory, started in China, was that this was a wholly man-made disease, created by Western powers in a US military laboratory; a bio-engineered "weapon" to wreak havoc on the Chinese and their economy.

As scientists around the world sought a vaccine, and various forms were being rolled out globally, further theories emerged. One example was that IT billionaire Bill Gates and his foundation had played a part in the disease's creation and were set to profit from any vaccine.

A FLU WORLD ORDER

QAnon, an American right-wing group who allege that there is a devil-worshipping, baby-eating pedophile ring consisting of Democrat politicians, Bill Gates, and entertainers such as Tom Hanks, also argue that Covid-19 is a lie, concocted by a Deep State of world influencers seeking ultimate control of all our lives, and that the former President Trump was battling alone against them.

During those protests in Germany and beyond in the summer of 2020, their "Q" sign was visible in the crowds and reports note that since 2019, their following in Europe alone has grown to 500,000. They argue that Covid-19 is a form of global state control, and that the information about the disease that is supplied to the world's population is a tool with which to gain that control. QAnon and those who share their beliefs argue that the death toll is fabricated in order to cause further panic and ultimately to wield power.

President Trump himself tweeted in October 2020 that Covid-19 was far less lethal than seasonal flu, which accounted for 100,000 deaths a year, and went on to argue that, "Our doctors get more money if somebody dies from COVID… I mean, our doctors are very smart people. So what they do is they say, 'I'm sorry, but, you know, everybody dies of COVID.'"

A short film released on various social media platforms called *Plandemic: The Hidden Agenda Behind Covid-19*, gained over 8 million views. In it, former research scientist Judy Mikovits stated that this was indeed a disease fabricated in a lab, that face masks make us sick, and that it could simply be cured by hydroxychloroquine (a medication used to fight illnesses such as malaria).

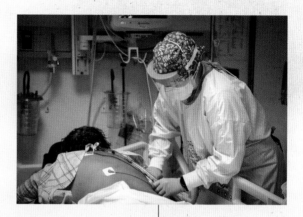

Hospitals all around
the world have been
struggling to cope with
the Covid-19 pandemic.

THE SKEPTICS

The key arguments put forward by the likes of QAnon and Trump and in
the UK Piers Corbyn, a British conspiracy theorist, are that Covid is not as
deadly as the flu, that this is not a pandemic, that lockdown is a tool to aid big
business and costs lives, and that the vaccine is a way of inserting microchips
into the population.

All have been disputed. Trump's seasonal flu figures were proven to be fake, the
global death rate proves this *is* a pandemic, that it is too early to truly analyze
the effects of lockdowns, and while Bill Gates has talked of "digital certificates"
after vaccines, the notion of microchips is nothing but science fiction.

Many others merely point to the thousands of heart-breaking reports that have
come from those working on the frontline. "Honestly, guys, it felt like I was
working in a war zone," Melissa Steiner, an ICU nurse in Michigan posted. "[I
was] completely isolated from my team members, limited resources, limited
supplies, limited responses from physicians because they're just as
overwhelmed… please take this seriously. This is so bad."

THE CURE
FOR CANCER

THE CONSPIRACY: ....MAJOR PHARMACEUTICAL
COMPANIES ARE HIDING
A CURE FOR CANCER

LOCATION: .... WORLDWIDE

Cancer has always been with us. Ancient Egyptian medical texts describe it, ancient Greek physicians wrote about it; even the might of the Roman Empire couldn't curtail it. Today cancer touches us all; somehow, every one of us will be affected.

In 1910, the US President William Howard Taft boasted that, "Within five years, cancer will have been removed from the list of fatal maladies," but defeating cancer is not comparable with dealing with a foreign power that wealth and powerful armies can destroy. Over 100 years later, cancer is still a fatal malady, but with all the wealth and technology at the world's fingertips, why is that so?

According to the American Cancer Society, there is an average of 1,660 deaths from cancer each day in the United States, that's 69 every hour. While it is true that huge progress has been made in research—and in some cases in curing the disease—these are numbers, mirrored all over the world, that raise questions about why over time medical science has not found a comprehensive cure for the disease.

Over a quarter of the American population are suspicious, believing that a cure has been found but it is being withheld, and that further research is being slowed down in order to facilitate the development of high-profit, single-use treatments, so some forms of cancer are currently curable—but not all of them.

The greed of "Big Pharma" companies is said to be the reason they've held back the cancer cure.

BIG PHARMA

The term "Big Pharma" has long been used by conspiracy theorists to describe the major pharmaceutical companies, who they feel have suppressed research for years across a number of diseases such as HIV and AIDS in order to continue to profit from the existing medications. It is Big Pharma's supposed involvement in the withholding of vital treatments for cancer that has caused the strongest reaction amongst conspiracy theorists.

The opponents of Big Pharma argue that medicines and treatments are becoming increasingly expensive, pointing out that ill health and disease, especially cancer, is big business. The theory is that the corporations, the regulators, politicians, and the non-governmental organizations involved are all in on the Big Pharma lie; that by a clandestine agreement they continue to hold back the science that the public blindly expects will one day help them and their loved ones.

The global pharmaceutical industry is a trillion-pound business and much of the enormous profit comes from pain relief, prevention drugs, and other treatments that assist in the fight against cancer. If there was a blanket cure for the disease, theorists believe that these corporations would lose a substantial proportion of their huge incomes. Add health insurance to that, plus the millions pumped into medical research, and a sudden and general change such as a comprehensive cure would cost the industry everything.

And it's not just the pharmaceutical industry acting alone; what many consider to be the even murkier worlds of politics and the media are also there to corroborate Big Pharma's actions and maintain the status quo, ensuring that a world without cancer is never realized.

THE SKEPTICS

Those charged with researching and developing medicines and cures for the many different cancers we are at risk from point to the fact that cancer is not just one disease, but hundreds of different types that can affect all parts of the body. Cures for some forms of cancer have been found, but not for others. They are not looking for a single cure, and therefore they cannot be hiding one.

Cancer survival rates have doubled in the last forty years. In the United States, over half of the people diagnosed with cancer in 2019 will survive for ten years or longer, due to giant steps taken in cancer research. The number of people working in the field is enormous and skeptics of the conspiracy point out that the Big Pharma companies—while needing to make money for their shareholders—are far from faceless entities, but have vast amounts of employees, so it would take a gigantic effort to keep a secret cure from the world. Dr. Robert Grimes, a respected Irish physicist and cancer researcher, published a paper in 2016 estimating that even if only the biggest companies in pharmaceuticals were in on the conspiracy, there would be around 715,000 people who knew something. With that many conspiracists, he argues, a whistleblower would have emerged.

Researchers, be they academics or those working commercially for the pharmaceutical corporations, are aware there is no "cure" per se, and there never will be. They work toward incrementally earlier detection of the disease, treatments that become more and more effective, and, in recent years, progressive preventative measures such as the HPV vaccine.

What can't be denied is that even if we believe that a blanket cure exists, the very important work being done by those in research and pharmaceuticals is driven by the need to put a stop to a devastating disease that is as old as humanity itself.

THE 2004 ASIAN TSUNAMI

THE CONSPIRACY: ......THE ASIAN TSUNAMI WAS CAUSED BY A MAN-MADE EXPLOSION BENEATH THE SEA

LOCATION: .... THE INDIAN OCEAN

DATE: .... DECEMBER 26, 2004

It was the day that paradise turned to hell. Amid the beauty of the Indian Ocean, hundreds of thousands of tourists on vacation began another lazy day by their pools or on the beach. Millions of locals began their working days. Fishermen cast their nets. Children played outside in the sunshine. What followed was a scene of destruction on a scale the world has rarely seen. Footage was beamed around the planet as the waves crashed in. Indonesia, southern India, Sri Lanka, and Thailand took the brunt but tidal surges were felt as far away as Western Australia. An apparent underwater earthquake caused nearly a quarter of a million people to lose their lives, but could the explosion that triggered this appalling tragedy have been man-made?

THE TSUNAMI HITS

Tsunamis are common in the Indian Ocean, but nothing had ever been seen of this incredible magnitude. Fourteen countries were hit by waves that crashed onto their shores and ripped through towns, villages, rural communities, and vacation resorts, destroying lives and tearing families apart forever as it went.

If this tsunami was caused by an earthquake, it was a massive one. Eventually it was estimated to have had reached a huge 9 on the Richter scale, but some geologists say it was even as high as 9.3. Its hypo-center (the earthquake or explosion's point of origin) was almost 100 miles off the western coast of northern Sumatra in Indonesia, at a depth of around nineteen miles below sea level.

It is the third largest earthquake ever recorded. For ten minutes (the longest recorded) it caused the Earth to vibrate as much as ten millimeters and is said to have triggered other quakes as far away as Alaska. But what if this wasn't a natural disaster?

In 1997, the then US Secretary for Defense, William S. Cohen, made a speech about a new kind of weapon. "Others are engaging even in an eco-type of terrorism whereby they can alter the climate, set off earthquakes, volcanoes remotely through the use of electromagnetic waves." Words that seven years later, after the devastation caused by the tsunami, set alarm bells ringing. Immediately after the wave withdrew and the full horror of its strength

Vast areas of southern Asia were wiped out after the tsunami of December 26, 2004.

became obvious, questions were asked. Why weren't locals warned? Why isn't a region so susceptible to earthquakes and tsunamis better protected against them? However, some asked questions about whether the seismic activity was actually created by those "eco-type" weapons, capable of causing underwater explosions and therefore creating nightmarish tsunamis.

Those suspicious minds turned their attention to President George W. Bush, and what they might see as his regime's desire to destroy a series of emerging economic markets in Asia, wash away terrorist organizations, and rebrand himself a hero in a region where anti-US sentiment was high after the repercussions of 9/11. After the tsunami, why had the United States sent a warship to the region? Why was a senior commander who had served in Iraq also sent? And wasn't it too much of a coincidence that this earthquake had struck exactly a year to the day that 30,000 people had died after an earthquake in Iran?

In 2006, the Egyptian weekly magazine *Al-Osboa* ran an article directly blaming US and Israeli armed forces for the nuclear explosion that caused the tsunami. Israel themselves had talked of their fears that Iran would one day be able to drop a device from an aircraft into the Mediterranean, 100 miles from Israel's coast, before detonating it underwater and causing a tsunami to hit. There was also precedent from the Second World War when as part of a program named Project Seal, the US Navy and New Zealand military attempted to develop tectonic weapons capable of destruction on this level. Testing was carried out in 1944, and then after the war in 1955 on a specific weapon, but between the end of the war and 1992 the United States alone carried out over 1,000 nuclear tests, the vast majority of them conducted underwater. If an explosion under the Indian Ocean wasn't a direct act of hostility, there are plenty of those who believe it was caused by these nuclear tests.

The United States also came under the spotlight when the huge death toll was finally revealed. The US naval base in the Indian Ocean had been notified of an impending disaster, giving them time to prepare and avoid casualties. It was an advantage not afforded to the communities that were so tragically decimated.

The island of Diego Garcia
in the Indian Ocean is the
site of a US naval base. The
base received prior warning
of the earthquake that
caused the tsunami.

THE SKEPTICS

"This was a natural disaster." So said Dr. Bart Bautisda, chief science
research specialist at the Philippine Institute of Volcanology and Seismology,
before disputing the idea that a weapon could be used to create the sort of
destruction the region had witnessed. "You would need a very huge amount
of energy," he said. "It's impossible. A billion tons could not do it... It's possible
to cause vibration, but not sufficient to cause disruption. We can tell the
difference between an artificial explosion and an earthquake. The mechanisms
are different."

THE
EPSILON TEAM

THE CONSPIRACY: ......A SECRET SOCIETY WITH
EXTRATERRESTRIAL ORIGINS
PROTECTS MODERN-DAY GREECE

LOCATION:.. GREECE

DATE: .... ANCIENT GREECE-PRESENT DAY

Mystery surrounds the existence of Epsilon, an alleged secret society
that is said to consist of prominent individuals who uphold the
ideologies of their ancient Greek ancestors. The eminent membership
is made up of philosophers, academics, business moguls, politicians,
and engineers—influential people who, through their membership of
this controversial group, have access to closely guarded knowledge
from an extraterrestrial source.

SECRET SOCIETIES

Covert groups have long been in existence; clandestine societies that strive to keep their activities and functions strictly confidential can be traced back through the centuries. Well-known but secretive organizations such as the Freemasons and the Mafia have for many years fascinated a public hungry to know more. It seems the less we know, the greater the intrigue.

In Africa, one such was the Crocodile Society, who supposedly practiced cannibalism. In Ireland, the Irish Republican Brotherhood was a secret, oath-bound fraternal organization dedicated to forming an independent Ireland. In England, the Bullingdon Club is a private, all-male dining club for students of Oxford University, its former members including David Cameron and Boris Johnson, both of whom went on to become prime ministers of Great Britain. For centuries, secret societies have met, thoughts have been shared, histories made, and politics affected, all under a veil of secrecy.

The Epsilon Team is thought to have been the creation of Spyridon Nagos, a Greek Freemason and socialist, who in the early twentieth century envisioned his own secret society of powerful and influential Greeks who

The School of Athens by the Italian Renaissance artist Raphael depicts and celebrates ancient Greek philosophy.

would develop ideas and work in secret, all for the benefit of their country. The modern mythology surrounding what would become the Epsilon Team stemmed from a 1977 book by George Lefkofrydis, *Spaceship Epsilon: Aristotle's Organon: The Researcher*. Inspired by ancient Greek philosophers such as Plutarch and Aristotle, Lefkofrydis developed various theories, one being that Aristotle was in fact an extraterrestrial being, and had left clues to his real identity in his collection of works on logic, *Organon*.

The term "Epsilon Team" came from the writer Ioannis Fourakis, who claimed that Greeks stem from extraterrestrial origins, citing old Greek mythology and tales of the Olympian gods. Today the society is still talked about, although no one knows if it is an urban legend or a real power base, capable of influencing the wider world.

Those who speculate about Epsilon say that their aim is to protect the Earth; that they want to keep alive ancient Greek values and belief in the old gods, declaring that mythology is vital to their way of life. They argue that Greek culture is superior to all others; that Greek DNA is unique due to the alien ancestors who have passed down knowledge through secret texts, including the key to advanced space travel. Their mission is to promote all positive aspects of Greece, including its art, culture, and languag; restore ancient moral codes; and to fervently defend Greece using science and technology.

MEMBERS

No one has openly admitted that they are part of the Epsilon Team, but prominent Greeks such as the shipping magnate Aristotle Onassis and his son, Alexander, have been suspected of being members (in Onassis Senior's case, he is thought to be a founder of the modern Epsilon Team in the 1950s) as have politicians, mayors, astronomers, and scientists.

In 1996, the society took a sinister far-right turn when *Omada E* was published, a bestselling book written by Anestis Keramydas, a former merchant navy officer. In it, he declared that he was part of the Epsilon Team and emphasized the group's belief in Greek domination, and that through their association with Greek gods and the Orthodox Church, Epsilon were here to fight a cosmic war against the Jewish race (who he claimed were also from extraterrestrial origin) and Jewish lobbyists around the world.

A bust of the ancient Greek philosopher Aristotle.

THE SKEPTICS

Organizations have affiliated themselves with the society but there are many inconsistencies, suggesting that one singular, organized group does not exist. In 2015, five men were arrested for the bombings of the Bank of Greece in Kalamata, a town in southern mainland Greece. The terrorist group called themselves "Team Epsilon," proclaiming themselves to be pagans aiming to "take down the conspiracy inflicted on Greece by the banks and by Orthodox Christianity."

Epsilon Team followers believe that Greek people and their culture have always been protected by the group, and that over the centuries that protection has enabled the country to thrive. Skeptics, however, argue that there was no sign of this protection in the country's darkest moments such as the 400 years of enslavement under the Ottoman Empire, the fall of Constantinople in 1453, occupation by Nazi Germany and Fascist Italy in the Second World War, or the financial crisis in 2008.

What is clear is those who study the Epsilon Team, whether they be authors, followers, or supposed members all have very differing versions of what the group represent and how they function, implying that it is more a way of thinking than an actual organization. Evidence suggests that Epsilon is an ideology shared by a group of intellectuals with an aptitude for deciphering ancient codes and writings inscribed on ancient ruins, and that the myth that Greece, its culture, and its population are protected by this group simply makes people feel safer and increases nationalistic pride.

THE SINKING
OF THE
RMS LUSITANIA

THE CONSPIRACY: ...... THE BRITISH ADMIRALTY
ARE IMPLICATED IN
THE LUSITANIA'S DEMISE

LOCATION: .... THE NORTH ATLANTIC OCEAN,
NEAR THE OLD HEAD OF
KINSALE, IRELAND

DATE: .... MAY 7, 1915

Enjoying a post-lunch stroll upon the deck of the lavish RMS *Lusitania* on a sunny May afternoon, Oliver Bernard noticed something approaching rapidly under the waves. It looked like the tail of a large fish, but with warnings prevalent of the dangers under these now war-torn seas, the young British theater designer suspected it could be a submarine.

Those suspicions became fear as a "streak of froth" made its way through the water, toward the ship. "This isn't a torpedo is it?" asked an American woman standing next to him. Less than twenty minutes later the ship had sunk, and 1,200 people had perished in the waters off southern Ireland. Germany would be immediately condemned for a heinous war crime, but they were not the only ones who had questions to answer. Could more have been done to prevent this tragic loss of life?

THE BACKGROUND

On April 17, 1915, less than a month before the sinking of the *Lusitania*, the German Embassy ran an advert in fifty US newspapers, including those in New York, from where she would soon depart on her voyage to Liverpool.

> "TRAVELLERS intending to embark on the Atlantic voyage are reminded that a state of war exists between Germany and her allies and Great Britain and her allies; that the zone of war includes the waters adjacent to the British Isles... vessels flying the flag of Great Britain, or any of her allies, are liable to destruction in those waters and that travellers sailing in the war zone on the ships of Great Britain or her allies do so at their own risk."

The seas of northern Europe had become an important theater of war when Britain established a naval blockade around Germany, ensuring nothing—not even food—was permitted to reach the enemy. Germany responded in early 1915, declaring the seas around the British Isles as a war zone and deploying U-boats (highly effective German military submarines) to potentially sink any ships it deemed a threat.

It took less than twenty minutes for the torpedoed ship to sink.

No matter; such was the demand for travel, ships such as the *Lusitania* continued on their commercial endeavors. But this voyage would end in tragedy. Just after 2 p.m., Captain Walther Schwieger ordered the firing of one torpedo from his U-20 that slammed into the *Lusitania*'s starboard side, right under her bridge.

Eighteen minutes later, while her passengers fought for their lives, the *Lusitania* lay broken at the bottom of the North Atlantic Ocean.

THE EVENTS

As the news of the sinking and the tragic civilian deaths spread, Germany was attacked for its callous act. *"The Huns Most Ghastly Crime!"* proclaimed an English newspaper, while the United States, the neutral home of 128 of the 1,198 people who perished, was horrified by what at first was simply seen as an act of wartime barbarity. But was it that simple?

Winston Churchill, the First Lord of the Admiralty, was always vocal in his desire to have the United States join the war. Prior to the sinking he had written a letter to Walter Runciman, the president of Britain's Board of Trade. In it, he said:

The young Winston Churchill's role in the sinking of the *Lusitania* has long been scrutinized.

"It is most important to attract neutral shipping to our shores in the hope especially of embroiling the United States with Germany... For our part we want the traffic—the more the better; and if some of it gets into trouble, better still."

With those words, Churchill invited the questions that followed. Of course, there could be no doubt that the *Lusitania* was sunk by the Germans, but what was the role played by Britain and indeed, Churchill? This after all was a disaster that eventually aided their war effort; the United States joined the war two years later.

Despite that condemnation of Germany, British authorities chose to also question the *Lusitania*'s captain, Bill Turner, criticizing his choices. Merchant ships were advised by the Admiralty to avoid headlands "near where submarines routinely lurked." They were told to instead steer a mid-channel course, to operate at full speed, and to "zigzag" in areas known to be dangerous.

But, the answers to the questions asked of Captain Turner actually turn the spotlight on the British Admiralty. The night before the sinking, Turner confidently said they would soon "be securely in the care of the Royal Navy." That care never came. On her last arrival in Liverpool (on the northeast coast of England) just weeks earlier, the *Lusitania* was escorted by two destroyers. But not on this occasion, despite four destroyers sitting idly on the nearby Welsh coast. The fact that no correspondence survived between Churchill and the First Sea Lord Jacky Fisher from the time of *Lusitania*'s last trip increased suspicion.

And then there were the dangers that the *Lusitania* was sailing into. From the time *Lusitania* had set sail from New York, twenty-three merchant vessels had been targeted in the same area off the coast of Ireland in which she perished. Turner was never informed and so chose not to zigzag or sail at top speed. An experienced naval man, had he known of the threat, he would surely have adhered to the Admiralty's advice regarding course and speed.

Speculation that this was an avoidable catastrophe increased over time, with radio exchanges between the *Lusitania* and the Admiralty made classified, fueling rumors that Turner had requested taking the northern route around Ireland into Liverpool but his request was denied, meaning he was forced to take this perilous course.

Another contentious issue was the two explosions reported by the U-boat captain and survivors. The British further chastised the Germans for firing two torpedoes at a civilian vessel, but Schwieger was adamant that he only sent one. The British had held back the fact that the *Lusitania* was carrying nearly 190 tons of rifle ammunition and 1,250 artillery shells among other flammable war materials. It was a fact that would explain the second explosion that caused her to sink so quickly, and was also used by the Germans for years after to justify the attack.

Nothing can condone such a loss of civilian life, but it seems that more could have been done to prevent the sinking of this great ship.

Many of the victims were buried in Queenstown in Ireland. The town has since been renamed Cobh.

THE SKEPTICS

Was the sinking of the RMS *Lusitania* a full-on conspiracy? Was it planned by the British? Both the evidence and common sense tells us that theory is impossible, especially when so much of the ship's fate came down to chance. Their late departure from New York, the slow pace in which Turner sailed her, a fog lifting allowing the U-boat to see her; none of these could have been planned.

But we cannot escape the fact that this was a commercial vessel, offered no protection in the most dangerous of circumstances, and therefore it is conceivable that the British felt that an injured *Lusitania* would simply have limped back into Liverpool, and provoked an American response.

If that was the case, they didn't account for that second, deadly explosion. Subsequent dives have confirmed that the British had lied and that there were indeed large amounts of munitions on board, ensuring that the ship was—in wartime terms—a legitimate target for German hostility, and while a 2012 study concluded that the explosion was caused by a boiler, there can be no doubt that at the very least, gross negligence on behalf of the British helped doom those on the *Lusitania* to their watery graves.

PONT-

SAINT-ESPRIT

CONSPIRACY: ....THE POPULATION OF A
FRENCH VILLAGE WAS
POISONED BY THE CIA

LOCATION: ....PONT-SAINT-ESPRIT,
OCCITANIE, FRANCE

DATE: .... AUGUST 16, 1951

In France they call the incident *Le Pain Maudit*; "the cursed bread."
On a warm, sleepy August day in the small southern-French village
of Pont-Saint-Esprit, a place where nothing out of the ordinary ever
happened, strange goings on began to take place. Swathes of the
population suffered intense physical and mental breakdowns. Of 250
cases, 50 locals ended up in an asylum and 7 people died. Criminal
action was taken against a local distributor of flour as the bread bought
from the village bakery was blamed for mass poisoning. For over half
a century, doubts have remained. Was this simply bad bread, or
something far more sinister?

THE STRANGEST DAY

Leon Armunier, the village postman, was that morning doing his rounds before suddenly feeling extremely nauseous. And then the hallucinations came. "It was terrible," he later said. "I had the sensation of shrinking and shrinking, and the fire and the serpents coiling around my arms." Mr. Armunier ended the day in hospital, in a straitjacket, surrounded by friends and neighbors chained to their beds. "They were thrashing wildly... screaming, and the sound of the metal beds and the jumping up and down... the noise was terrible."

One person spoke glowingly of the heavenly choruses he heard and the beautiful colors he saw. Another wrote pages and pages of dazzling poetry. These, however, were the lucky ones. For the vast majority affected, this was an apocalyptic day. "I have seen healthy men and women suddenly become terrorized, ripping their bed sheets, hiding themselves beneath their blankets to escape hallucinations," said Albert Hébrard, the mayor of Pont-Saint-Esprit.

A man jumped from his window to escape snakes. A couple ran amok in the street, fighting each other, armed with knives. A girl fled through the village streets to escape from tigers. A man broke up his furniture to make weapons to fight off the horrific beasts that were pursuing him. A distraught mother told passersby that her children had been made into sausages. Dogs bit stones and ducks marched like penguins. Another, believing himself to be a circus act, attempted to cross the Rhône by balancing on the cables of a nearby suspension bridge. But what had caused such mass hysteria?

A CRIMINAL ACT?

Three days after the mayhem ensued, police concluded that those affected had been poisoned by batches of bread, sold by the local bakery Roch Briand. Briand's owner was interrogated; locals were questioned. Some said that their bread had a strange chemical smell, a smell consistent with a bad odor given off by those rendered sick, leading investigators to Maurice Maillet, the supplier of the bakery's flour. In time, he was charged with involuntary manslaughter for trading in improper ingredients.

The unchallenged view for decades after that bizarre day in southern France was that it was caused by negligence. But then, in 2009, an investigative journalist called Hank Albarelli wrote a book called *A Terrible Mistake: The Murder of Frank Olson and the CIA's Cold War Experiments*, looking at the Central Intelligence Agency's use of substances and mind control experiments after the war.

Dr. Frank Olson was a CIA scientist and agent who headed up their studies into the research of LSD (lysergic acid diethylamide, a powerful hallucinogenic drug). In his book, Albarelli discovered a CIA document that read: "Re: Pont-Saint-Esprit and F. Olson Files. SO Span/France Operation file, inclusive Olson. Intel files. Hand carry to Belin—tell him to see to it that these are buried." Albarelli firmly believed that the CIA were experimenting with mass poisoning using LSD, and that they dosed the townspeople of Pont-Saint-Esprit by infecting the village's bread.

Two years later, Frank Olson fell from a Manhattan hotel window. Suicide. But there are those who suggest he himself was drugged, that as a result of the growing tensions between the United States and the Soviet Union plus the onset of the Korean War, the CIA was looking into biological warfare, and that "field experiments" using drugs such as LSD were the worrying norm around the world. Project MKUltra, headed up by Dr. Sidney Gottlieb, was the CIA program that looked closely at LSD and how it could be used in warfare. The official line after the criminal investigation was that ergot fungi had infected and tainted the grains used to make the village's bread, poisoning anyone who consumed it.

But by using Freedom of Information legislation, Albarelli uncovered another CIA report from 1954. In it, an agent documented a conversation with an employee at the Sandoz chemical company in Switzerland, less than 300 miles from Pont-Saint-Esprit and the only place where LSD was being produced at the time. "The Pont-Saint-Esprit 'secret' is that it was not the bread at all," the employee said. "It was not grain ergot."

An ergot fungus called *Claviceps purpurea*, shown here, was given as the cause of the events in Pont-Saint-Esprit.

THE SKEPTICS

Plenty of experts agree with a report that appeared in the *British Medical Journal* soon after the outbreak, supporting the theory that the incident was brought on by ergot fungus and that *Claviceps purpurea* (ergot) produces alkaloids similar to LSD. US academic Steven Kaplan responded to allegations that LSD was used, stating that the symptoms did not fit the drug, and that there was no chance it could have survived the temperatures in the baker's oven. Albarelli suggested that it might have been added to the bread after baking.

The two men might disagree, but they have both stated publicly that the French government should open an inquiry to find out what actually happened on that summer's day in Pont-Saint-Esprit.

THE PHILADELPHIA EXPERIMENT

THE CONSPIRACY: ....THE US NAVY TRIED TO
MAKE THEIR SHIPS INVISIBLE

LOCATION: ....PHILADELPHIA, PENNSYLVANIA,
UNITED STATES

DATE: .... OCTOBER 1943

The world's future is in the balance. A planet ravaged by four years of catastrophic warfare is still no closer to knowing who will emerge from this unprecedented conflict as victorious. By the late summer of 1943, the Allies and their enemies were desperate to try any solution to gain an upper hand. Increasingly, radical innovations in science and technology were being sought to provide the much-needed military advantage that might just tip the balance.

Earlier that summer, Adolf Hitler had approved plans to build the new V-2 rocket, the world's first long-range, guided ballistic missile. The United States and their allies needed to counter the potential advantage given by such weapons of mass destruction, and so it is said plans were made for a top-secret experiment that could render their naval fleet invisible. This became known as the Philadelphia Experiment.

THE BACKGROUND

That same summer, American troops led by General Patton took the Italian island of Sicily. It was a vital victory, one that President Roosevelt described as "the beginning of the end." The Germans fought back with massive air strikes, but with the Mediterranean now opened up, it was a victory that underlined the vital role the Navy would play if the Allies were to win the war.

In America, strenuous efforts were being made to gain a military advantage. Albert Einstein coined the term "unified field theory" to describe his attempt to combine his general theory of relativity with electromagnetism (what some referred to as electromagnetic space-time warping).

This theory generated speculation as to whether somehow using large electrical generators to cause the bending of light around an object via refraction could make it invisible, however large it was. Sources reported that the US Navy secretly sponsored the project, hoping success would win the battle on the oceans and therefore hasten the end of the war.

The naval shipyard in Philadelphia where the strange experiments were allegedly carried out.

THE EVENTS

The USS *Eldridge* was a new but unremarkable-looking addition to the US naval fleet. As part of Project Rainbow, in the summer of 1943, the vessel was fitted with the necessary scientific equipment at the Philadelphia Naval Shipyard. Testing was said to have gone well, until on one occasion eyewitnesses spoke of a "greenish fog" enveloping and seeming to replace the ship before lifting and returning the *Eldridge* to its place in the yard.

But what had happened to those on board? Some crew supposedly suffered with severe nausea but more incredibly, it was reported that one man on board was found with his hand lodged in the steel hull of the vessel. Undeterred, the Navy repeated the experiment on October 28, and on this occasion it is said that the USS *Eldridge* not only disappeared, but also appeared to onlookers 200 miles away in Norfolk, Virginia.

Crew on the SS *Andrew Furuseth*, a merchant ship, witnessed this before the *Eldridge* once again vanished, reappearing in Philadelphia but at a terrible cost to those on board. Limbs were once more fused to the ship's bulkheads, bodies horribly turned inside out, some crew simply never reappeared, while surviving crew suffered with terrible mental disorders; all were "brainwashed" into forgetting the experiment ever happened, and therefore ensuring the truth never came out.

Ten years after the end of the war, letters from a man named Carl Allen, using the pseudonym Carlos Miguel Allende, were sent to science fiction writer Morris K. Jessup. Jessup had written in his books on UFOs that anti-gravity and electromagnetism would provide more effective propulsion for space vehicles than rocket fuel, prompting Allende to admit to witnessing the Philadelphia Experiment while aboard the SS *Andrew Furuseth*.

Jessup took his own life in 1959, but Allende's testimonies lived on, gaining traction and interest along the way, giving this strange individual a cult-like status among conspiracy theorists. Some even believed that he was in fact an alien himself, involved in a cover-up regarding the Navy's involvement with extraterrestrials.

It was a peculiar twist in a peculiar tale, but Allende's claims as an eyewitness were enough to have created a phenomenon that sparked fictional adaptations, and forced the US Navy to answer some difficult questions.

The USS *Eldridge*—an unremarkable ship with a remarkable story.

THE SKEPTICS

While much of the supposed goings-on at the Philadelphia Naval Yard in the summer of 1943 can be filed under "extraordinary," talk of the experiment and its incredible fallout was enough to garner interest from the world of publishing (a 1978 novel named *Thin Air*) and Hollywood (the 1984 movie *The Philadelphia Experiment*), plus further coverage in the musings of coauthors Charles Berlitz and William L. Moore, prolific writers on mystery and conspiracy.

The Navy admitted they were trying to make their ships "invisible to radar" but Allende's state of mind was questioned, his timings of where and when ships were based used to discredit his story. Edward Dudgeon, a naval crewman, spoke to UFO investigator Jacques Vallée about a procedure where vessels were wrapped in large cables and high voltages were sent through them in an attempt to scramble the ships' magnetic signature, rendering them undetectable to enemy radar.

A remarkable story that despite overwhelming evidence to discredit the facts, still intrigues today. Perhaps the tale of the Philadelphia Experiment will never disappear, unlike the USS *Eldridge*?

BLACK HELICOPTERS OVER THE USA

CONSPIRACY: ....THERE IS A CLANDESTINE
POLICE FORCE AND A NEW
GOVERNMENT POISED TO TAKE
OVER THE UNITED STATES

LOCATION: .... UNITED STATES

DATE: .... 1970S-PRESENT DAY

From the witch trials of Salem in the sixteenth century, to the fear of domestic communism and the McCarthy trials that soured the 1950s, through to the modern post-9/11 America and the anxiety-inducing politics of Donald Trump, paranoia and the dread of infiltration from within has dominated the fears of many citizens of the United States.

To some conspiracy theorists, the sightings of black helicopters hovering over the lives of everyday Americans are merely linked to UFOs, but there are those who feel they indicate the presence of an insidious and looming military force. There are many who believe that the helicopters are an undeniable sign of an outside power keeping watch, a clandestine military force monitoring their target, gathering information as they ready themselves for invasion.

In the 1970s, unexplained and unmarked black helicopters were spotted flying low over areas of agricultural America. The federal government had been investigating strange cases of seemingly motiveless mutilation of cattle, and there was growing speculation as to whether there could be a link with these aircraft. Christian theorists (fueled by the evangelist Hal Lindsey's 1970 book, *The Late, Great Planet Earth*) referred to the Book of Revelations in the New Testament, suggesting that the plague of locusts in the Bible were represented in the modern world by these helicopters, alluding to an impending Armageddon.

In the 1980s there were hundreds of reports from all over the country, from men and women claiming to have been harassed and spied on by these same black helicopters, and it was now that speculation grew that the aircraft could indicate the possible presence of a confidential police force. Some maintained that a secret government was taking shape and those unwilling to cooperate would be severely dealt with.

Into the 1990s, perhaps influenced by TV series such as the hugely popular *The X-Files* and the 1997 movie, *Men in Black*, the helicopters in that same color took on a new extraterrestrial twist. Was there an actual government agency charged with the cover up of alien life? It has been suggested that reported sightings of the helicopters were usually near supposed UFO hotspots.

The plot thickened, but the niceties of unexplained flying objects in the twenty-first century have been overtaken by a more serious proposition put forward by militia groups. They allege that the United States will soon be under attack by outside forces, who will take over and run the country, and that the helicopters are paving the way by spying on and monitoring those who might oppose them.

WHO'S LOOKING DOWN ON AMERICA?

One theory is that crews flying these helicopters, also wearing unmarked black uniforms, are part of a highly classified CIA project that involves the training of selected and ultimately indoctrinated assassins. Trained to kill, these agents seek out and eliminate those who might obstruct a new government. Others talk of a secret brotherhood run by international bankers, suggesting that those flying the crafts are their armed guards, or that the helicopters in fact are seen hovering over the sites constructed by government agencies in the event of a looming nuclear war.

A sinister line of thinking is that the United States is indeed under threat from a New World Order, and that the United Nations, using these helicopters to police the country, will soon take over America and then the rest of the world. Extreme Christian theorists again look to the Book of Revelations and concur that the Antichrist and his global domination will actually rise from the UN.

Less religious theories look at the UN and its "Agenda 21/2030 Mission Goals," that according to some include plans for a one-world government; a single, global cashless currency; a global army; the end of private ownership; mandatory microchipping; and, amid the global coronavirus pandemic, it is suggested that there is a very real plot by the UN to wipe out 90 percent of the world's population.

The United Nations was set up
to maintain peace and security,
but many fear it is instead
hell-bent on global control.

Are they simply helicopters on patrol or something far more sinister?

THE SKEPTICS

This is a conspiracy theory that is so widely known it has seeped into everyday American life and its rhetoric. When addressing the National Rifle Association's concerns about compulsory background checks, the now President Joe Biden said: "The black helicopter crowd is really upset. It's kind of scary, man," alluding to the militia's fear that their gun rights and other freedoms are in fact under threat.

The helicopters themselves have been attributed to many homeland organizations such as US Customs and Border Protection, who employ a dozen UH-60 Black Hawk helicopters, or the US Army's 160th Special Operations Aviation Regiment, who regularly fly their dark-colored helicopters on stealth exercises and training maneuvers.

While far-right organizations such as the American Policy Center have derided the UN and its 1992 Agenda 21/2030 statement as "a new kind of tyranny that, if not stopped, will surely lead us to a new Dark Ages of pain and misery yet unknown to mankind" (APC president Tom DeWeese), to many it is a force for good. Merely an innocent old mission statement that maps out a plan for the environment, world peace, and the ending of child poverty.

CHEMTRAILS

THE CONSPIRACY: .... GLOBAL POWERS ARE SPRAYING CHEMICAL ELEMENTS FROM AIRCRAFT TO CONTROL THE ENVIRONMENT

LOCATION: .... WORLDWIDE

DATE: .... 1996-PRESENT DAY

Have you ever looked up at an airplane flying high and noticed the long vapor trails that linger in the sky after it has passed by? While we might think of these trails as a safe by-product, there is a growing belief that they are being purposefully designed to cause harm, not only to the environment but also the general public.

The aviation industry calls them condensation trails ("contrails"), made up mainly of water that has formed into ice crystals at high altitude. Not so, says a growing movement that is claiming these are actually chemical trails ("chemtrails"), released from jet engines by global powers seeking to manipulate the weather and thereby control events across the world.

What has become a global concern began in the United States in 1996, when the US Air Force published a report on weather modification, prompting an outcry from environmentalists and fears that mysterious and dangerous substances were being used by high-flying aircraft. As the rumors spread, national environmental agencies and those in federal aviation felt compelled to counter these stories by producing fact sheets to establish the truth. This flat denial only turned more heads toward the sky.

WHAT ARE CHEMTRAILS?

Those who believe in chemtrails distinguish them by their lengthy duration. Unlike normal airplane trails that disappear quickly, these more sinister examples, first seen in the mid-1990s, persist for up to half a day and then turn to cirrus-like cloud cover.

Suzanne Maher, a Canadian who founded the Bye Bye Blue Sky organization that raises awareness of the phenomenon, believes that everyone needs to take notice of what is happening above us. "I ask that we move beyond the notion that this is a conspiracy theory," she says. "Twenty to thirty years ago we never saw these trails. We had a beautiful blue sky."

According to chemtrail believers, the toxic trails left behind in our skies are a dangerous cocktail of aluminum, strontium, and barium, released into the atmosphere to control weather for "military purposes and global domination." Further theories suggest these chemicals are being used to manage population figures by enforcing mass sterilization, and a reduction in life expectancy. Chemtrails are also aiding chemical and biological weapon testing, damaging crops to manipulate stock prices, and helping giant pharmaceutical companies who would be in a position to exploit the various illnesses caused for their own profit.

WHO IS BEHIND THEM?

While suspicions were first raised in the United States, this is very much an international movement. In a recent international survey, 17 percent of respondents believed in the existence of a "secret large-scale atmospheric program."

Geo-engineering, the deliberate intervention in the Earth's natural systems, is said by authorities to be a force for good and is used to counteract climate change. However, officials argue this is still very much in the research stage. Not so, say chemtrail believers. They claim that as far back as 1932 the Soviet Union opened The Leningrad Institute of Rainmaking, and that in 2008, the Chinese authorities used cloud seeding (the modification of precipitation coming from the cloud) to ensure the opening ceremony of the 2008 Olympics wasn't affected by heavy rain.

Today, it is thought that various governments are behind these chemicals being released, and that powerful families are investing in this area in the hope of dominating environmental issues. The Rothschilds, a long-established dynasty who made their huge fortune in European banking in the 1700s, are said to be prominent figures within the chemtrail conspiracy. In 2011, a branch of the Rothschild empire bought a controlling stake in Weather Central, a provider of weather forecasts to hundreds of broadcasters all over the world. "As weather becomes more extreme around the planet, with greater human and financial ramifications," Sir Evelyn de Rothschild said in a positive press release, "we believe that Weather Central will play a major role in mitigating damage and improving lives." The Rothschild name is no stranger to conspiracy theories; the family has been blamed for wrongdoings throughout history from the assassination of President Abraham Lincoln to the bankrolling of Adolf Hitler. There are observers who see their movement into the field of weather as an opportunity to create and then profit from natural disasters.

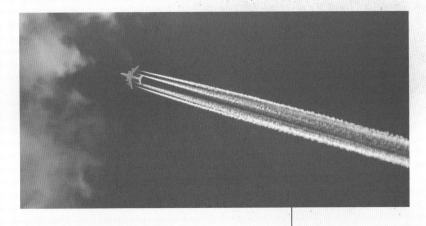

Are the trails
left by the world's
airliners helping
to control the
planet's weather?

THE SKEPTICS

The US Air Force has been compelled to answer its critics and categorically deny strategic weather modification systems, adding that it has no plans to explore them. "They would say that" is the obvious response, but international independent scientists concur. Recently, seventy-seven scientists and experts in atmospheric science studied the evidence; seventy-six found no evidence of a secret large-scale atmospheric program, and in addition stated that "The data cited as evidence [for such a program] could be explained through other factors, including well-understood physics and chemistry associated with aircraft," suggesting that the trails are very simply the natural result of aviation.

There are scientists who are calling for further research into geo-engineering, arguing that it is a necessity to obstruct global warming and that solar geo-engineering, involving the atmospheric aerosol injection of tiny reflective particles, can reduce the amount of sunlight reaching the Earth and thereby cooling an overheating planet.

THE DEATH OF OSAMA BIN LADEN

THE CONSPIRACY: .... THE US GOVERNMENT
                 MISLED THE PUBLIC ABOUT THE
                 DEATH OF THE AL-QAEDA LEADER

LOCATION: ....ABBOTTABAD, PAKISTAN

DATE: .... MAY 2, 2011

On the night of May 2, 2011, almost ten years after the terrorist atrocities of 9/11, President Barack Obama walked along the deep, red carpet toward the White House's East Room where he would address the nation.

"Tonight," the president said, "I can report to the American people and to the world that the United States has conducted an operation that killed Osama bin Laden, the leader of al-Qaeda and a terrorist who's responsible for the murder of thousands of innocent men, women, and children."

It was a speech that brought justice and closure to many who remained shell-shocked by the tragic events of 9/11. But, while many Americans gathered outside the White House and at Ground Zero, where the Twin Towers once stood, singing "U-S-A! – U-S-A!" triumphantly, many others had their doubts.

OSAMA BIN LADEN IS DEAD

Hand-in-hand with the grief and shock felt around the world after 9/11 was a tangible anger and the desire for revenge. Osama bin Laden, the leader of al-Qaeda, was the main orchestrator of the atrocities and while he remained in hiding, his face became one of the most widely recognized on the planet.

With a $25 million FBI bounty on his head and CIA agents working for years in the shadows trying to locate the terrorist leader, intel of a courier used by bin Laden led to a compound in Abbottabad, Pakistan.

Surveillance of the compound lasted for months. Satellite cameras were unable to make a firm identification of bin Laden inside the compound, but using high-tech spyware, information was passed on that this was likely to be the hideout the United States had been looking for. "It was a fifty-five/forty-five percent proposition," Obama later admitted and such was the doubt around who was there and in the surrounding area, the president, fearing civilian casualties, refused to sanction the use of a drone or missile to wipe out the whole building.

9/11's Ground Zero, where the hunt began for bin Laden.

"U-S-A! U S A!" Crowds gather outside the White House the night President Obama told the world they'd gotten bin Laden.

Instead, Operation Neptune Spear was given the green light. Under the cover of night, twenty-three Navy Seals were flown in aboard Black Hawk helicopters (one crashed on landing), breached gates and doors with C-4 charges (a plastic explosive), engaged in a firefight, killed their target, took the body, all without the Pakistani government knowing, finally allowing the president to tell the world they had got their man.

THE DOUBTS

On May 4, 2011, the Obama administration announced that they would not be releasing any photographic evidence of bin Laden's body prior to its reported Islamic burial at sea, and immediately suspicions were aroused. Firstly, the probability of successfully carrying out the operation was deemed improbable. Sending twenty-three Seals into hostile Pakistani airspace without air or ground cover seemed suicidal, and if this really was bin Laden's hideaway, surely it would be heavily guarded? No local police were ever involved, in spite of the fact that a Black Hawk helicopter had crashed, and the whole affair was conducted without the knowledge or support of Pakistani intelligence services.

Soon, an administration under interrogation was changing vital details of the raid. Bin Laden was not armed and there had been no firefight; bin Laden had not used his wife as a human shield and there had been no live footage relayed back on helmet cameras.

With these doubts came suggestions of motive. The presidential election was only a year away, and this was a chance for Obama to appear as the bold leader who had delivered the nation's public enemy no.1. He also wanted to start the phasing out of troops from Afghanistan, a step made much easier by announcing victory over al-Qaeda. It was further argued that bin Laden

The president and his team (including Hillary Clinton, who is covering her mouth) watch footage of the Navy Seals operation. The idea they were watching live has since been questioned.

had in fact died long before 2011. Hamid Gul, of the Pakistani Inter-Services Intelligence (ISI), immediately said, "They must have known that he had died some years ago so they were waiting. They were keeping this story on the ice and they were looking for an appropriate moment and it couldn't be a better moment because President Obama had to fight off his first salvo in his next year's election as he runs for the presidency and for the White House and I think it is a very appropriate time to come out."

Closer to home, US investigative journalist Seymour Hersh published a 10,000-word report heavily disputing the government's account. "The story stunk from day one," he said. In his report, using prominent special operations sources, he stated that in fact the Pakistanis allowed US helicopters into their airspace and that they cleared the compound of guards prior to the Seals' arrival. He claimed that bin Laden's death was going to be announced a week later as part of a drone strike on a mountain range near the Afghan border, but that the president's hand had been forced by the crashed Black Hawk helicopter, making it impossible to keep the raid a secret.

Twenty-three Navy Seals were sent into bin Laden's Pakistani compound. Pakistani leaders say it would have been impossible without their permission.

Osama bin Laden's
death will continue
to be debated, and the
official version of
events will certainly
continue to be
scrutinized.

THE SKEPTICS

The question of bin Laden's conveniently quick burial at sea was what most fueled doubts about his death, but the administration's counter-argument was that the body had to be buried immediately in line with Islamic tradition, and that as it was at sea, there could be no "terrorist shrine."

Similarly, the administration had refused to release photographs of bin Laden's body as proof of the killing, not only because of their disturbing nature, but it was also feared that by doing so they would be inviting retaliatory attacks from sympathetic terrorist groups.

4

THE
HISTORY
BOOKS

For centuries historians and theologians have sought the truth, but what if that truth cannot always be found, cannot always be definite? As far back as ancient Egypt and ancient Greece, questions have been raised by those seeking more than what they were told. Here we will open those history books and seek our own answers. Was much of the fifteenth-century life of France's Joan of Arc a myth, was Alexander the Great murdered in 323 BC, and have we really walked on the Moon?

THE MOON
LANDINGS

THE CONSPIRACY: .... NASA AND THE US
GOVERNMENT FAKED THE MOON LANDINGS

LOCATION: .... JOHN F. KENNEDY SPACE
CENTER, FLORIDA, UNITED STATES

DATE .. JULY 20, 1969-DECEMBER 11, 1972

The Moon has always held a unique significance for humankind, whether that be as the ruler of the ocean tides, observed as a timekeeper, a compass or a calendar, or revered as a god. On a night in mid-July 1969, the Moon represented a finishing line. The United States was sending men to explore the lunar surface, and therefore winning the Space Race that had consumed two new superpowers for over a decade.

As the astronauts Neil Armstrong and Buzz Aldrin took their (and humankind's) first steps on the Moon's chalky surface, the world was watching. But did it believe what it saw?

"ONE GIANT LEAP"

Those were Neil Armstrong's iconic words as he stepped from Apollo 11 onto the Moon's Sea of Tranquility. Nearly 300,000 miles away on Earth, there are plenty who to this day think it was one giant lie.

What started with one man's theory, published in a modest pamphlet, has morphed into a belief in what is arguably the world's biggest and most extravagant cover up. Half a century later and the notion exists that all six manned missions to the Moon were nothing but a hoax designed not to take humanity further into space, but to win a cold war being fought on Earth.

The Space Race between the United States and the Soviet Union began in the mid-1950s. On October 4, 1957, the Soviets launched the first ever satellite, Sputnik 1, into orbit. Three years later, Russian cosmonaut Yuri Gagarin became the first human to be launched into space. The battle was on, but its backdrop was the ballistic missile-based nuclear arms race between the two

In 1958 the Soviet cosmonaut Yuri Gagarin, pictured here, became the first man in space, yet eleven years later the United States won the race to the Moon.

nations, and the symbolic battle between East and West after the Second World War.

The Moon was that symbolic finishing line, but by the time the last US mission there returned to Earth in 1972, the world had become a more rebellious place. The Watergate scandal was erupting in Washington, the president himself could no longer be trusted, while the Vietnam War, raging in Asia, had a whole generation vocalizing their distrust of power.

And then in 1976, a man called Bill Kaysing, a former employee of a company that designed the Saturn V rocket engines, self-published a pamphlet named *We Never Went to the Moon: America's Thirty-Billion Dollar Swindle*. It was a modest little tome, but in it Kaysing argued that there was no way NASA (National Aeronautics and Space Administration) could have successfully landed men on the Moon, let alone got them home again. With it, a conspiracy theory was launched.

ONE GIANT LIE?

While small in size, Kaysing's pamphlet started to gain big attention. In it he argued that NASA was an organization struggling to keep up with the Russians; that it was facing humiliation and the $30 billion it raised in funding was used to pay off conspirators. Looking at the landing itself, he questioned the absence of stars in the lunar surface photographs, claiming that NASA chose not to include them as astronomers would be able to tell any photos used were in fact taken from Earth.

Suddenly there were more questions being asked. Why was there an anomaly with the shadows seen in the photos? How were there footprints when there is no water on the Moon? The angle and the color of the shadows differed, suggesting that artificial lights were used, and why on landing the lunar modules, were there no blast craters? Also, the rockets should have on descent generated huge dust clouds near their landing sites.

A more sinister angle to Kaysing's pamphlet looked at the death of Thomas Baron, a quality control safety inspector for North American Aviation (contractors for NASA) who leaked a report critical of safety standards, citing the Apollo 1 fire in 1967 that killed all three crew members. Just days after testifying to a NASA review board, Baron was himself killed in a car accident. Kaysing, who would reiterate his views until his death in 2005, later went on to accuse NASA of deliberately causing the 1986 Space Shuttle Challenger disaster as members of the crew were going to expose the lunar cover-up.

In 1980, the Flat Earth Society, unwilling to believe that space travel is possible, also accused NASA of faking their lunar achievements, this time citing outside organizations and individuals as being involved. Disney it was said sponsored the operation, while the science-fiction writer Arthur C. Clarke produced the script, and Stanley Kubrick, already much praised for the sets on his movie *2001: A Space Odyssey*, directed the footage from a top-secret Hollywood studio.

To add to suspicions of the conspiracy, in that same year Kubrick made the horror movie *The Shining*. On closer inspection of the film, academics have seen clues to Kubrick's involvement with the filming of the faked landings.

In photos of Apollo 11 on the lunar surface, the shadows, the lack of stars, and the movement of the fl ag were all cited as evidence of a cover up.

Danny, the small boy in the movie, wears an Apollo 11 jumper, but more subtle are the ideas that the number of the haunted room, 237, actually alludes to the mean distance of Earth to the Moon, that the carpet pattern in the hotel is the same as the Apollo launch pad, and that the speech Jack delivers to his wife, Wendy, about a duty of work and honoring a contract is in fact an admission of the director's guilt at keeping such a grave secret.

Today, despite space travel very much remaining part of modern life and footage of Mars being beamed back to Earth, the question of the faked Moon landings won't go away, and modern platforms are giving a voice to the doubts. Podcaster Joe Rogan and controversial YouTuber Shane Dawson have aired their suspicions, and in a recent poll carried out among twenty-one to thirty-five-year-olds in the UK, 21 percent agreed that the Moon landings never happened.

A young Stanley Kubrick is thought to have directed the faked Moon landings, and you can find plenty of clues in his 1980 movie, *The Shining*.

"One giant leap for mankind," were Neil Armstrong's famous words, but were they one giant lie?

THE SKEPTICS

In 2002, a thirty-eight-year-old man from Tennessee called Bart Sibrel approached a group of astronauts and US hero Buzz Aldrin and called him a liar, a coward, and a thief. Sibrel received a punch in the face for his comments but no matter, he continued to argue that the Moon landings were a "Cold War, CIA, and Nixon administration deception," and that he had compelling evidence to prove it.

That evidence was no different than what had come before and, while no more punches have been thrown, counter-arguments—the cameras focused on the foreground missing what would have been very faint stars, that shadows on the Moon are complicated by reflected light and uneven ground, and the fact the footprints are amazingly still visible due to the lack of wind are among them— have constantly been offered, as have the facts that the Moon rocks brought back have been analyzed by third parties and found to be genuine.

No matter though, doubters remain and over fifty years since the world first looked up in awe at what was happening on that Sea of Tranquility, a far less tranquil debate rages on.

ROSWELL

THE CONSPIRACY: .... THE US AIR FORCE
DISCOVERED ALIEN LIFE

LOCATION: .... ROSWELL, LINCOLN COUNTY,
NEW MEXICO, UNITED STATES

DATE: .... JULY 1947

"RAAF Captures Flying Saucer on Ranch in Roswell Region." On July 8, 1947, the *Roswell Daily Record* ran this front-page headline. Something had crashed from the sky on a ranch seventy miles north of the city of Roswell. The headline made a change from the usually sleepy news in this quiet, military region of New Mexico, but in time it lit a fire under what has become the most famous, most researched, and most scrutinized sighting of extraterrestrial life this world has ever known.

A STRANGE DISCOVERY

In the mid-summer of 1947, a rancher named William Brazel, making his usual rounds on the J. B. Foster ranch in New Mexico, noticed some debris on the ground. "A large area of bright wreckage made up of rubber strips, tinfoil, a rather tough paper, and sticks," was how he described it at the time. Intrigued by recent local gossip about "flying saucers," Brazel wondered about his discovery and so took it to Sheriff George Wilcox in Roswell, and "whispered kinda confidential like" that perhaps what he had found was from outer space.

The sheriff was equally fascinated. What were these strange materials? He reported them to Colonel William Blanchard, the commanding officer of the Roswell Army Air Field (RAAF) who sent agents to the ranch for further investigation. With gossip beginning to turn to speculation, the RAAF released a statement: "The many rumors regarding the flying disc became a reality yesterday when the intelligence office of the 509th Bomb Group of the Eighth Air Force, Roswell Army Air Field, was fortunate enough to gain

Major Jesse Marcel was the chief intelligence officer at Roswell and examined the recovered debris.

Official reports from Roswell
changed quickly, and it was said,
unconvincingly, that they had in
fact recovered a weather balloon.

possession of a disc through the cooperation of one of the local ranchers and
the sheriff's office of Chaves County."

That was enough for the local newspaper. Their "flying saucer" story ran,
gained some interest, and raised some eyebrows. Yes, locals talked about
the supposedly mysterious disk, but eventually the story went quiet. US
Army officials had dampened the hype with a new statement suggesting
the articles found were in fact part of a weather balloon, even having an
army major photographed with some of the debris as proof. And that was
that. For now...

THE EVENTS

In 1978, the "Roswell incident" found its way back onto a newspaper's front page; this time the *National Enquirer*, bringing the story to a newer audience and sparking further investigation into top-level cover-ups and the very real idea that the US Army and government had in fact concealed not only a crashed UFO, but had found, studied, and retained three alien creatures.

In 1980, a book was published. *The Roswell Incident* sold 160,000 copies and in it the authors, Charles Berlitz and William Moore, having spoken to over ninety new witnesses, stated that in the summer of 1947 an alien craft was flying over New Mexico observing the United States's nuclear activity when it was hit by a bolt of lightning and crashed, killing the alien life on board and triggering a three-decade cover up.

Among those ninety witnesses were the individuals involved or directly connected to the events some thirty years earlier. Bill Brazel, the son of the rancher and present when the debris was discovered, the Brazels' neighbor Floyd Proctor, and Walt Whitman, the son of W. E. Whitman, the newsman who had interviewed Mr. Brazel in 1947, all testified in the book. As did Major Jesse Marcel, the man photographed with what the military said were the remains of a crashed weather balloon. Now though, Marcel and the others told *their* truth. The major, when asked about what he had first seen, described the debris as "nothing made on this earth." Brazel and the others agreed saying that the materials they found had a super-strength to them, not compatible with anything like a weather balloon.

And to add to the now persistent accusations of a cover up, the book and the testimonies within it told of how the press weren't permitted close inspection by the military at the time and that it was then swapped for materials found on weather balloons. Suddenly the tone was very different from those twee headlines in the local paper all those years before. There were accusations of intimidation toward those witnesses and even the incarceration of Mr. Brazel, the rancher.

The book also introduced new witnesses such as Barney Barnett, a civil engineer, who with a group of archeology students saw the wreckage and stated that it was indeed that of a strange aircraft and even more shockingly, that they saw dead bodies alongside it.

Through the 1980s, the book and the many others that followed it gripped readers in the United States and beyond. New witnesses, who had seen an unidentifiable object in the area, came forward. Those bodies that Barnett and the students had seen were unanswered for until in 1989, Glenn Dennis, a former mortician told of a colleague who had worked at the Roswell Army Air Field. There they had accidentally walked into the wrong examination room and witnessed doctors working on three bodies; bodies not recognizable as human, describing them as having small torsos, spindly limbs and large, bald heads.

These were no longer mere ramblings; no longer sensationalized gossip in the *National Enquirer*. Whatever had happened in the skies over New Mexico in the summer of 1947 had not been fully disclosed and the US military and government had questions to answer. The Roswell Incident would not go away.

Suspicions around what actually happened at Roswell all those years ago continue to circulate.

THE SKEPTICS

In 1994, the government, pressed on why back in 1947 the RAAF had changed their statement, admitted that the story about the debris coming from a weather balloon was in fact bogus. Instead, they said, it was the wreckage from a spy device involved in a classified project called Project Mogul. High-altitude balloons equipped with microphones were designed to float over the Soviet Union, monitoring the testing of atomic bombs. So covert was the operation that they had to offer a false explanation. Plenty didn't believe them.

And what of those bodies? In 1997, they were explained as merely crash test dummies, in a report that the authorities hoped would draw a line under the whole affair. Case closed? Some agreed. Roger Launius, a historian and retired curator for the Division of Space History at the Smithsonian National Air and Space Museum, said, "Has absolutely every question been answered? I can't say that. But I'm not sure that there are significant holes... My surmise is they probably saw [the initial flying saucer explanation] as a useful cover story."

But this is Roswell and the more the powers-that-be cover their tracks, the more those who believe in the secrets that lie there are skeptical. Donald Schmitt, a UFO researcher who has spent nearly three decades investigating the incident and is the cofounder of the International UFO Museum and Research Center in Roswell, argues that the original flying saucer account was far too flamboyant, and too likely to draw attention to an area home to sensitive military operations to have been used as a mere cover story.

"Two hours west of Roswell the first atomic bomb was detonated. You had ongoing atomic research at Los Alamos. You had all this testing of captured German V-2 rockets at White Sands. And at Roswell, you had the first atomic bomb squadron headquartered," Schmitt says. "The thought that they would have intentionally set up any type of publicity as a distraction? If anything, they needed less attention."

When it comes to Roswell, that attention may never go away.

THE DEATH OF ALEXANDER THE GREAT

THE CONSPIRACY: ......THE KING OF MACEDONIA
                        WAS MURDERED

LOCATION: .... BABYLON

DATE: .... JUNE 323 BC

Alexander the Great's prowess as a king and a military leader is indisputable. Ruling over the ancient Greek kingdom of Macedonia from 336–323 BC, Alexander spent much of his short reign pursuing a military campaign on an unprecedented scale to create one of the largest empires in the ancient world, extending from Europe through western and northeastern Asia.

What is less certain is how Alexander died. Aged just thirty-two, his death in the ancient city of Babylon in southern Mesopotamia (present-day Iraq) continues to intrigue historians. Was his demise due to natural causes or was it foul play?

THE BACKGROUND

In 323 BC, Alexander the Great lay dead in the palace of Nebuchadnezzar II in Babylon. The king of Macedonia, Alexander was the greatest military leader the world had ever seen and was mourned by his generals and subjects alike. Had a life of hard drinking and battle caught up with him? Many felt it wasn't as simple as that.

Plutarch, a Greek philosopher and historian, wrote that fourteen days prior to his death, Alexander had entertained an admiral named Nearchus before continuing his revelries with a friend, the commander Medius of Larissa. He then developed a fever that intensified rapidly and took away his speech prior to his death.

Diodorus, another ancient Greek historian, sees it differently. He argued that Alexander was in fact laid low after drinking excessively from a bowl of "unmixed wine" (wine was usually diluted with water in ancient Greece) in honor of the Greek hero, Heracles. What followed was eleven days of agony, no fever but a painful death.

A mighty general! Alexander the Great was revered for his military campaigns that saw him rule vast swathes of Europe, the Middle East, and Asia.

Both accounts leave the actual reasons for Alexander's death as up for debate. Natural causes have been cited. Alexander liked to drink and liver disease is a possibility, as are malaria and typhoid, but what of murder? There are those who insist the great king was assassinated.

In ancient Macedonia, murder was a frequent occurrence, and while Alexander was hugely popular, it would be naive to think that a leader who spread his empire so far and wide, winning so many bloody battles, would not have enemies. This was a theory supported by many of the ancient historians. Justin, a Roman historian from the third century AD, argued that the king was indeed the victim of a poisoning conspiracy, and even placed a Macedonian general named Antipater as the hatcher of the plot.

Antipater had served under Alexander's father but their relationship was said to be fractious, that the king became jealous of his general's victories. Antipater had been removed as a Macedonian viceroy, and is said to have plotted, possibly with Alexander's former tutor, Aristotle, to poison the king. Antipater's son Iollas was Alexander's wine pourer, so perfectly placed to deliver the poison. It's a theory that is backed up, even in the present day.

In a 2003 documentary aired in Britain investigating the death of Alexander, Dr. Leo Schep from the New Zealand National Poisons Centre argued that the deadly plant white hellebore (*Veratrum album*) was used. White hellebore was widespread and known to be deadly during Alexander's reign. Dr. Schep later made the powerful case that the plant's poison has a prolonged effect that fits with accounts such as that of Diodorus.

Paul Doherty, in his book *Alexander the Great: The Death of a God*, argued that Alexander was killed by his illegitimate half-brother, Ptolemy I Soter, a supposedly trusted companion who it is said used arsenic in Alexander's wine. While Ptolemy acted quickly to bury Alexander after his death and lay claim to succeed him (Alexander never named a successor), and by doing so highlighted his ambition, the theory that it was arsenic is contested by modern scientists such as Schep who point out that the prolonged nature of Alexander's illness was not in line with the effects of that particular poison.

So, the mystery and the arguments continue. Alexander's greatness is not in doubt, but the realities that surround his death most certainly are.

While Alexander never lost a battle, he had plenty of enemies who wished him dead. Was he murdered?

THE SKEPTICS

Alexander the Great lived a full life. Dying at such a young age, those who question the notion that he was killed unnaturally point to a larger-than-life figure who drank excessively, who never lost a battle but suffered many wounds. The fact that he survived so many potentially fatal blows in battle further heightened his god-like status. But despite his great strength Alexander was flesh and bone, and vulnerable to infection and disease like any other human. It has been suggested that his death could be attributable to West Nile fever, a disease spread by mosquitoes and affecting the elderly and those with a weak immune system, but there are questions about whether the virus was infecting humans before the eighth century.

Other diseases that certainly were widespread at that time were malaria, typhoid (both common in Babylon), meningitis, and spondylitis. There is also the possibility that the king's heavy drinking might have caused liver damage and acute pancreatitis. When a study of his symptoms was entered into the Global Infectious Disease Epidemiology Network, it was influenza that came out as the highest probability.

Malaria; the flu; too much wine. All might have ended a great life, but poison is also a strong possibility. We may never know, and can only speculate what Alexander might have achieved if his reign had not come to such an untimely end.

ADOLF
HITLER'S
ESCAPE

THE CONSPIRACY: ....HITLER AVOIDED THE
ALLIES AND LIVED IN ARGENTINA

LOCATIONS: ....BERLIN, GERMANY; ARGENTINA

DATE: 1945-1962

All around him was death. On the streets of Berlin outside the
underground bunker in which Adolf Hitler hid away, Soviet mortars
flattened the city. Their snipers picked out the ever-shrinking
number of loyal soldiers fighting on in his name. The city and the
people he hoped his Third Reich would rule over for 1,000 years
were being destroyed.

Beyond the crumbling city, Europe burned. Hitler, and the evil
ideology he hoped would suffocate the world, were facing defeat. The
war that had rumbled on for six years was nearly over, and the notion
that he would be taken captive by those he so detested was as repulsive
to him as the defeat he refused to accept.

Hitler then disappeared. Suicide by gunshot and cyanide was the
official story, but there are those who disagree.

HITLER'S LAST DAYS?

Unwell and unwilling to concede defeat, the last days of Adolf Hitler's war were spent in his Berlin bunker. There he stood over maps of Europe, a continent he had destroyed but which he ultimately couldn't conquer, which in his view was the fault of his generals, whose treacherous cowardice had so failed him.

On medication, and looked after by personal staff and his girlfriend Eva Braun, Hitler listened as Russian shells got louder and closer with every day. The Führer had retreated to his bunker in January 1945. Russian troops had advanced across Poland and by early April, 2.5 million of them were surrounding the German capital. By mid-April, they had reached the city center, and were fighting Hitler's dwindling army just yards from the bunker.

Even Hitler knew that beyond the walls of the bunker, defeat was certain. He dictated his final will to his personal secretary, Gertrude Junge, and married Braun in front of witnesses. That night he and Eva, Goebbels and his wife Magda, and Hitler's private sectary Martin Bormann celebrated the wedding, talking of the good times in their lives. He lined up his entire staff and shook

Europe rejoices in 1945. The war was definitely won, but did Hitler really die?

their hands, wishing them well and thanking them for their service, and in the early hours of the next morning, on hearing that Mussolini and his mistress had been executed by partisans, Hitler reiterated that he would never be taken prisoner by the Russians. The following day, Adolf Hitler and his new wife were no longer in the bunker...

AN ESCAPE

Suspicions regarding Adolf Hitler's fate emerged just a month after VE (Victory in Europe) Day, and the question marks came not from idle talk, but from the very powers that had defeated him. On June 9, 1945, Soviet Marshal Georgy Zhukov held a press conference and having been briefed by his leader, Joseph Stalin, when asked by journalists how Hitler died, stated that he was in fact "living in either Spain or Argentina."

Charred remains of a body had been discovered close to the bunker but in newspaper reports, the British quoted Russian sources that said it actually belonged to that of a "very poor double." As early as 1944, the US secret service had published pictures of how they imagined Hitler might look if he disguised himself before attempting to escape, and after the war the US media followed the UK, quoting one Soviet commandant who was adamant that, "Hitler had gone into hiding somewhere in Europe."

The war was won but the fate of its most evil protagonist was very much on the minds of people everywhere, and public opinion on what had happened was split. In 1947, 51 percent of Americans polled believed Hitler was actually alive. Popular opinion may have shifted over the seven decades since the end of the war, but today there remains a significant amount of suspicion that Hitler's death in 1945 was indeed a hoax.

In 2014, a book named *Grey Wolf: The Escape of Adolf Hitler* was published. In it, its coauthor historian Gerrard Williams argues that, "There's no forensic evidence whatsoever to suggest that Hitler or Eva Braun died in the bunker. There is a huge amount of contemporary news reporting to say that he escaped and made it to Argentina where he lived until 1962."

Official reports state that Hitler and Braun, having said goodbye to their staff, took themselves to their private quarters. There, Braun took a

The shallow grave near
the bunker, where it
was said that remains
of Hitler and his wife
were found.

cyanide pill, while her new husband shot himself. Not so, say Williams and other historians.

Instead of killing themselves and asking for their bodies to be burned, Hitler and Braun, knowing the network of bunkers below the streets of Berlin and helped by Martin Bormann, made their way from the bunker and emerged miles away where a Luftwaffe pilot named Peter Baumgart was waiting to fly them to Denmark, then on to Spain, where Fascist leader General Franco had made arrangements for a long submarine journey under the Atlantic to Argentina.

Baumgart actually testified in court that he flew Hitler and Braun to safety in 1945. There have been plenty of sightings of Hitler in Argentina, living in a

Germanic community, surrounded by other "ex-pats." The theory goes that, aided by Argentine leader Juan Perón, as payback for the large financial donations the Nazis gave his regime, Hitler lived out his life in a Bavarian-styled mansion, before dying alone in 1962 (Braun is said to have left him in 1954 with their daughter, who they named Ursula).

Perhaps the most compelling evidence came in 2009 when a US television show examined fragments of a skull found near the bunker in 1945, kept in Russian federal archives and thought to be that of Hitler. One fragment did show signs of a gunshot wound, but the scientists who performed DNA and forensic tests on it found that it actually belonged to a woman under forty.

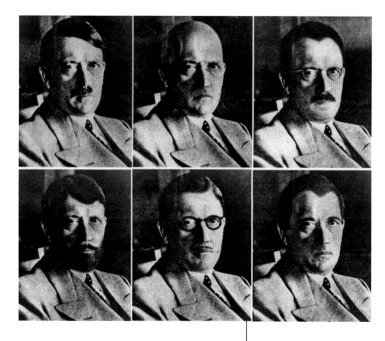

The US Office of Strategic Services commissioned an artist to mock up images of Hitler in disguise, in the event that the dictator tried to flee from justice.

His Third Reich
failed and his war
was lost, but the
mystery surrounding
Adolf Hitler's death
rages on today.

THE SKEPTICS

Despite a West German court in the 1950s finding enough hard evidence to rule that Hitler did indeed commit suicide in Berlin, and despite eye-witness accounts such as that of his personal secretary Gertrude Junge agreeing that he and Eva Braun did kill themselves, the theory that Hitler escaped and lived out his life on another continent continues to thrive.

Between 2015 and 2018, the History channel broadcast a series called *Hunting Hitler*, based on the dictator's survival. Each episode attracted an average of 3 million viewers worldwide, underlining the continued fascination with the fate of Adolf Hitler—a fascination that many historians argue can blur the lines of reality. Evidence such as the fragments of skull are interesting, but counter evidence tells us that a section of a jawline was also found that did in fact match Hitler's dental records. The pilot who testified that he had flown Hitler to safety has been discredited because he needed "psychiatric evaluations," and the sightings of Hitler in Argentina have been put down to imposters seeking financial reward.

There is also an argument that Hitler, even after the war, was a political tool, and that the continued suggestion that he had escaped was perpetuated by the Soviet Union who, entering the new Cold War, wanted to discredit the West for allowing the world's most notorious monster to avoid justice.

Whether Adolf Hitler did die in that bunker or did indeed escape, it seems clear that the world's fascination with his evil is very much alive.

THE
BISLEY BOY

THE CONSPIRACY: .... ELIZABETH I WAS A
                            MALE IMPOSTER

LOCATION: .... BISLEY, GLOUCESTERSHIRE, UK

DATE: 1542

Queen Elizabeth I. A Tudor monarch. The daughter of Henry VIII.
She stands resplendent in a grandiose and opulent gown, adorned by
jewels. The ruff around her neck is as iconic as the crown that sits upon
that fiery head of red hair. She has a knowing look as she gazes out
at her subjects.

Reigning over England from 1558 to 1603, in a tenure known as "The
Golden Age," her country enjoyed fabulous economic prosperity,
relative peace compared to her predecessors, and what war she did
face, she did so victoriously with her famous triumph over the Spanish
Armada. This was a queen whose story and achievements would be
celebrated for centuries to come; that image of her ingrained in a
nation's consciousness. But, this was a quiet, almost secretive and
mysterious monarch. She herself would say "*video et taceo*" or "I see
and keep silent."

But what if she was harboring her own secrets? What if this strong and
silent queen was an imposter?

"I know I have the body of a weak and feeble woman, but I have the heart and stomach of a king, and of a king of England too." Queen Elizabeth I's famous words on August 9, 1588, were delivered to her troops as they prepared for a possible Spanish invasion.

But there is a school of thought that, decades earlier, the individual making that speech had been introduced as a surrogate for the dead Princess Elizabeth—and that the surrogate was in reality a man.

THE EVENTS

In 1542, aged nine years old, the young Elizabeth, daughter to King Henry VIII and his second wife, Anne Boleyn, was sent to a small village in Gloucestershire called Bisley. Life at court in London had become dangerous with the outbreak of the bubonic plague. While she was not then in line for the throne, she was very dear to the king, and her health and safety was

Princess Elizabeth was the much-loved daughter of King Henry VIII and his second wife, Anne Boleyn.

Thomas Parry and his wife Anne were said to have carried out the cover-up. He was later knighted and buried at Westminster Abbey by Queen Elizabeth.

important to him. Especially as one day soon she could be married off to a foreign kingdom such as France or Spain in order to cement relations between fractious nations.

But Elizabeth never left Bisley. Staying at an old hunting lodge known as Overcourt House (it still stands today), it is said that while there, Elizabeth did become ill and consequently died. The king and his wife had put their daughter in the care of two guardians, Sir Thomas Parry and Lady Kat Ashley, and so fearful were they for their lives, they decided to not tell the king and instead conspired to find a girl in the village who could replace Elizabeth, an imposter who would fill in and deceive him.

They acted quickly as the king was due to visit in a matter of days. They buried the body in an unmarked grave near the house, set off into the village but could not find a girl to be their imposter as none had the same fair complexion. There was, however, a petite young boy with a physique similar to that of the princess who they dressed in girls' clothes and a wig, successfully fooling the king on his arrival. And so this boy was taken from his village to live his life as a princess, and ultimately as the Queen of England.

As Elizabeth, the boy settled into his new royal life, his secret kept resolutely by Sir Thomas Parry and Lady Kat Ashley, those with the most to lose should the secret ever come out. As a princess, Elizabeth began to fit into her surroundings, being seen at the right functions, saying the right things, learning about the world. In fact, her tutor, Roger Ascham, was so enamored with his pupil he said, "The constitution of her mind, is exempt from female weakness, and she is embued [sic] with a masculine power of application."

With time, Elizabeth became queen, a strong figure who ruled with less brutishness than her father, but with equal rigor. Those who adhere to the conspiracy point to her appearance. Very much aware of her image (Elizabeth was very particular about her portraits) and always in elaborate wigs, it is said that the queen refused to be seen in public without heavy white makeup and a ruff around her neck. Could the makeup be there to conceal any stubble, and could the ruff be doing the same, while also covering male traits such as an Adam's apple?

It may seem far-fetched but there are historians who give the story their time. Many point to the fact that Elizabeth remained single and didn't have

The iconic image of Queen Elizabeth I, but were the ruff and the heavy makeup she wore used to cover her true identity?

any children, despite that fact meaning the end of the house of Tudor. Elizabeth had many admirers, proposals of marriage came from all over Europe, but the queen stated that she was and would always be married to her country. Was this merely a ruse; was Elizabeth in fact shunning prospective admirers purely to keep the secret? A secret she shared only with Sir Thomas Parry and Lady Kat Ashley, who became firm and close advisers during her reign. In 1589, one nobleman, a Sir Robert Tyrwhitt, suggested there was an unknown secret between the trio, and said of the closeness between them, "There's a pact between them to take that secret to the grave."

Elizabeth's marriage to England ended when she died aged sixty-nine in March 1603, but the nature of her death and burial further fueled the flames for those who believe in the story. No autopsy was ever performed and instead of a grand and lavish funeral befitting such a longstanding and well-loved monarch, her bones were simply interred with her sister Mary's in a grave in Westminster Abbey, London, that to this day has never been breached. Over 400 years later, and there are some who question who is really buried in that grave.

Bram Stoker, the author
of *Dracula*, wrote a
story about the Bisley
Boy in 1910.

A LITERARY LEGACY

In 1910 Bram Stoker, the author of the hugely successful novel, *Dracula*, published another story called *Famous Imposters*. In it he told the story of the Bisley Boy, a tale he had heard from locals on a visit to Bisley. When he noticed the May Day queen there was actually a boy dressed up, and heard the reasons for the tradition, plus the fact that his friend who lived there, the Reverend Thomas Keeble at Overcourt House, had found the skeleton of a child dressed in girls' Tudor clothing befitting the child of a rich and powerful family, he had to put it on paper. It was another success—but for the majority of historians, the idea that a male imposter lived the life of a princess and then a queen is as fanciful as any vampire story.

THE MARRIAGE OF JESUS

CONSPIRACY: ....DESPITE THE BIBLE'S
TEACHINGS, JESUS WAS MARRIED

LOCATION: ....NAZARETH AND JERUSALEM
(IN MODERN-DAY ISRAEL)

DATE: .... CIRCA 25-30 AD

While there is no concrete physical or archeological evidence for
his existence as an individual, Jesus of Nazareth's teachings have
influenced life in all four corners of the world for 2,000 years. Through
gospels and parables we have been told of the miracles of Jesus. Water
turned into wine, the lame able to walk again, the hungry fed. What we
know nothing of is how he lived his everyday life, what his upbringing
was like, his schooling, how he gained access to the Hebrew Bible
(Tanakh), who his teachers were, or whether he had a romantic
relationship or became a father.

THE BACKGROUND

According to the Gospel of Luke (2:41–2:51), aged twelve years old, Jesus traveled to Jerusalem with his parents to celebrate Passover. That is it. That is the only thing the Bible tells us about his life from the age of eight days old, until his early thirties.

The idea that Jesus was married has long been mulled over within Christian ideology. As far back as the first century, the Gnostic scriptures indicate that Jesus was in a romantic relationship. These ancient writings, unearthed in Egypt in the 1940s, study the development of early Christianity and give a different account of the beliefs of Jesus from that revealed in the New Testament.

What is widely agreed is that if we were to discover that Jesus had married, it should not come as a shock. History tells us that to marry and father children was very much expected of Jewish men. All four gospels call Jesus "Rabbi," and Rabbis were married. If Jesus hadn't been married, it would have raised eyebrows, scandalizing his family; and the Bible does talk of a woman in his life, Mary Magdalene, a disciple and witness but also his wife.

There is no doubt that Mary Magdalene was a close disciple of Jesus, but many theologians argue that she was much more than that.

MORE THAN A FOLLOWER?

In the Gnostic Gospel of Philip, Mary is referred to as Jesus's "companion" and it is said that he "kissed her often," going on to suggest she was closer to Jesus than any other apostle. "The Savior loved you above all other women," the gospel tells us that Peter said to Mary.

Mary Magdalene was, according to Western theologians, a prostitute, a ruined woman who Jesus saved, casting out her demons before she became part of a small group of women who traveled with him. The downplaying of Mary's morals and therefore her role in Jesus's life is a pattern among those unwilling to accept that he had a relationship or a marriage, but it is clear she was more than just one of many followers.

According to the Gospel of John, Mary was present at the crucifixion of Jesus, sitting at his feet and, once all his other disciples had fled, she is said to have visited the tomb alone to find it empty. John also says that Jesus appeared to Mary and told her to tell the disciples that he had returned.

"Mary Magdalene is among Jesus's early followers," says Robert Cargill, assistant professor of classics and religious studies at the University of Iowa. "She was named in the Gospels, so she obviously was important. There were apparently hundreds, if not thousands, of followers of Jesus, but we don't know most of their names. So the fact that she's named is a big deal."

Is it more than that? In 2014 a book was published titled *The Lost Gospel: Decoding the Ancient Text that Reveals Jesus' Marriage to Mary the Magdalene*. The text is based on what was found in the rare manuscript section of the British Library where it sat for the past 160 years, and is ostensibly about the biblical Joseph, and his wife Aseneth. In the Syriac community, however, from which this gospel emerged, "Joseph" was a stand-in for Jesus, and Aseneth is Mary, going on to say that she "had many children by the Crucified."

In addition to the book, in 2015 a fragment of an ancient papyrus was discovered and the words written in Coptic, "Jesus said to them, 'My wife'" as well as "... she will be able to be my disciple," and carbon testing on the papyrus suggested it was written between the fourth and eighth centuries, and authentic.

Mary was present at the crucifixion of Christ, and the Bible says she remained with him while other disciples fled.

THE SKEPTICS

When Dan Brown's 2003 novel *The Da Vinci Code* went viral around the world, the question of whether Jesus's bloodline truly existed (a key plot line in the novel) once again reared its head. Those in the Church and beyond have long chosen to disbelieve any talk of Jesus's matrimony and fatherhood, pointing to it as more akin to Brown's fiction than any kind of studied reality.

Martin Scorsese's movie *The Last Temptation of Christ* also caused a stir when it was released in 1988. It starts with a disclaimer that reads, "This film is not based on the Gospels, but upon the fictional exploration of the eternal spiritual conflict," but it didn't matter. The exploration of Jesus, the actual man, is contentious and while the film played in the world's movie theaters, terrorist attacks (a Catholic group attacked a theater in Paris), death threats (Scorsese was threatened by Evangelists), and protests (hundreds of people marched on Universal Studios) illustrated the depth of feeling that it generated.

JOAN OF ARC

CONSPIRACY: .. THE LIFE STORY OF FRANCE'S
                PATRON SAINT IS A LIE

LOCATION: .... FRANCE

DATE: 1412-1431

In her native France, Joan of Arc is a national symbol of resistance and hope, the iconic focal point of the Hundred Years' War between England and France (1337–1453). In the Catholic Church she is canonized, her short life celebrated nearly 600 years after her execution. During the First World War, while shells dropped and death consumed their comrades, French soldiers kept her image in their jacket pockets, there to offer hope in the mud and despair. There to remind them of their nation's courageous spirit.

Seemingly communicated to by God, the story of Joan of Arc's bravery against the English and her subsequent death continues to enthrall us. But was hers a life misrepresented? Was she, in fact, not who she claimed? Was she even executed by the English? The Hundred Years' War was eventually won, but this debate has raged for even longer…

FIERCE LOYALTY

The story of Joan of Arc and her short life remains very much part of a modern narrative. In May 1920, she was made Saint Joan of Arc in Paris's Notre Dame Cathedral. Sixty thousand people attended the ceremony, with the President Raymond Poincaré saying, "In her spirit, let us remain united for the good of Mankind."

Around 1412, Joan of Arc was born to Isabelle Romée and her husband Jacques, a tenant farmer, in the village of Domrémy in northeastern France. Joan was never taught to read or write, but influenced by her mother's religious beliefs, she became a devout Catholic. Conflict raged around them. What was later known as the Hundred Years' War was very much ongoing as Joan grew up, and despite her village being surrounded by pro-English and pro-Burgundian influences, her family was fiercely loyal to the French crown.

Joan of Arc remains revered in her native France and within the Catholic Church.

Joan of Arc meets with King Charles VII. The painting today hangs in the Louvre Museum in Paris.

The war though was very much going against that crown. A peace treaty in 1420 had disinherited the French crown prince, Charles of Valois, and King Henry V was made ruler of both England and France, a title inherited in 1422 by his son Henry VI. Joan's village was often attacked and many were forced to flee.

A CALL TO ARMS

It was aged thirteen that Joan first started to hear voices. She would state that it was while sitting in the garden at her family home that she witnessed visitations from three saints, Michael, Margaret, and Catherine, telling her to drive out the English and to install Charles as France's rightful king.

Convinced of her divine mission Joan took a vow of chastity, refused an arranged marriage organized by her father, and instead, in 1428, made her way to Vaucouleurs, a stronghold for those loyal to Charles. Despite the expected cynicism, Joan gained a small following, those who believed in an old prophecy that foretold of a virgin destined to save France.

With her hair cut short and dressed in men's clothes, Joan made an eleven-day walk through enemy territory, persuading Charles to let her lead an army to Orléans, a town long under siege. It was there, on her iconic white horse, that Joan's attacks forced the Anglo-Burgundians from their bastion to retreat over the Loire River.

Joan's reputation and power (advisers to Charles suggested she had too much of the latter) grew as she continued to take the battle to the pro-English forces, but in the spring of 1430, having fallen from her horse, she was taken captive by Burgundian forces at Compiègne.

Joan of Arc is seen as a military icon, but she never partook in battle.

Imprisoned, ignored by Charles, accused of heresy and witchcraft and impersonating a man, Joan of Arc was burned at the stake in Rouen, northern France on May 30, 1431. She was nineteen. Admiration for this remarkable young woman and her extraordinary bravery increased over time and eventually, twenty years later, she was posthumously pardoned by Charles VII.

THE LEGACY

A statue of Joan of Arc stands in Paris's Notre Dame Cathedral, and for so many in France, the notion that her story is somehow fabricated—or worse, falsified—is too much to bear. Many French medievalists debunk the doubters, suggesting they are merely titillated by *Da Vinci Code*-esque investigations. Claims that Joan in fact avoided execution have long been discussed but historians are on the whole satisfied that she was—thanks largely to the records of the trial of nullification (a retrial to investigate the outcome of Joan's original trial) which contain sworn testimony from several witnesses present at the execution, who confirmed the identity of the defendant as that of Joan of Arc.

Politically, the country's far right refuse to belittle the figure that the likes of Jean-Marie Le Pen use as a symbol of the nation's purity and bravery, while the far left also fights hard to reclaim Joan's memory, suggesting her politics would have matched their own.

A French historian, Olivier Bouzy, recently scoffed at all claims. "These theories have been knocked down a hundred times," he said. "This is about people who are not historians, who don't understand the mentality of the Middle Ages, looking for a contemporary explanation. It shows there is a clear market of readers who aren't satisfied with what history tells us, otherwise [their] books would never be published."

THE SKEPTICS

Scholars and historians have taken issue with her cult status and the facts that surround her life and possibly faked death. In the early twentieth century, the Catholic Church resisted calls to canonize her, suggesting that her claims to have been sent by God must be false as she was captured; they cited her signed abjure when threatened with death (she later took it back, leading to her execution), and they questioned her claims to be a virgin.

There are questions that continue to be asked in the modern day, and investigative journalist Marcel Gay and former secret service agent Roger Senzig argue that this was not a peasant girl taking messages from heaven, but actually an illegitimate daughter of the French queen consort, Isabeau of Bavaria, and that she was actually groomed to be a political puppet. They claim she was in fact manipulated in a cover up they call "Operation Virgin."

Educated, taught English, trained for battle, Joan was far from touched by God, and it was in fact her grasp of English that saved her from burning at the stake. Senzig and Gay believe that instead of burning there, Joan escaped, another woman was killed, and she married a French knight, Robert des Armoises. "Everything they taught us at school," Marcel Gay told an English newspaper, "was wrong."

As far back as 1436, just a few years after Joan of Arc's supposed death, a Jeanne des Armoises came forward saying she was Joan, gaining gifts and subsidies, while duping powerful nobles along the way. Eventually she met with Charles VII of France and as she didn't know the secret that Joan had supposedly revealed to him on their first meeting, thereby convincing him that she had been sent by God to lead the French to victory against the English, Jeanne was forced to admit that she was an imposter.

ODESSA

THE CONSPIRACY: ....ODESSA HELPED NAZIS ESCAPE JUSTICE AFTER THE WAR

LOCATION: ....GERMANY, EUROPE, AND SOUTH AMERICA

DATE: ....(DISPUTED) 1944 OR 1947

The summer of 1945. The war is over. Six years of the most devastating conflict the planet has ever seen, but with the surrender of Germany in May and then that of Japan in August, the world can turn its attention to the future. Or can it?

Europe and vast parts of Asia are under rubble, 75 million lives have been lost, and the horrific extent of the crimes committed by Adolf Hitler's Nazi regime are yet to be fully realized. While Hitler is reported to be dead, those who served under him, those members of his SS (*Schutzstaffel* or Protection Squads) and Gestapo would need to be brought to justice.

The likes of Adolf Eichmann, the architect of the Final Solution (the genocide of the Jewish race), and Joseph Mengele, the notorious doctor at Auschwitz, would not come quietly. Instead they hid, used powerful contacts and fled justice to start new lives in far-flung lands. But who aided their escapes?

AN ESCAPE ROUTE

After 1945, the time had come to attempt to restore peace and stability amid the burning embers of war still alight all over Europe and beyond. That meant not only clearing the visible destruction caused by six years of unprecedented annihilation, but also bringing those guilty of the most heinous war crimes to justice.

With swastikas coming down all over Europe, some suspects were rounded up for trial, but there were many who fell through the cracks. However, they needed an organization to fund them, to get them access to credible paperwork such as identification papers, and to provide them with new lives elsewhere—South America or the Middle East—where they could regroup and maybe, in time, even resurface. That organization was ODESSA.

After the war, thousands of Nazi generals faced trial, but plenty escaped. How?

NAZI SYMPATHIZERS

ODESSA derives from the German: *Organisation der ehemaligen SS-Angehörigen* or Organization of Former SS Members. Some say it was formed in 1944 by SS leader Heinrich Himmler, an opportunist who felt the war was being lost and that soon he and other high-ranking Nazis would need safe passage from the Allies. Others say that in 1947, leading former SS and Gestapo members met near Odessa in Ukraine to discuss secretive escape outfits that could aid not only the safety of its members, but hopefully one day reignite Hitler's war and realize a "Fourth Reich."

Immediately after the war, the emphasis was on creating an actual network, set up to provide Nazi escapees with access out of Europe to the safety of countries in South America and the Middle East. Reliable and safe contact points would be set up every twenty-five miles, meaning a cloister route out of Germany, either to the southwest through Spain or south through Genoa in northern Italy, and down to Rome before sailing from Europe to a new world, predominantly in South America.

As well as aiding escape, ODESSA would also work to hamper those charged with bringing Nazis to justice, and offered to—should a case against a member come to court—provide financial help, ensuring the best defense money could buy. With cells operating throughout Germany in the majority of its major cities, the word spread, clandestine meetings were set up in hotels and cafés, individual escapes were planned, and operations coordinated, along with a neo-Nazi future where the party's plan could eventually be fully realized.

With that in mind, the Nazi Party had stored and could call on untold riches, from the implementation of the Final Solution against Europe's Jews and the wealth taken from them, to the vast array of treasures, art and gold stolen over their time in power and secured in banks in neutral countries such as Switzerland.

Additional wealth could be ascertained by using contacts in the criminal underworld and arms left over from the war were swapped throughout the Arab world for opium and marijuana, prior to deals being set up with certain Mafia organizations with contacts in the world's now booming drug trade. ODESSA could rely on friends in high and powerful places, as well as those

The Argentine President, Juan Perón, is said to have aided senior Nazis fleeing Europe after the war.

in criminal circles. Commercial groups such as the Red Cross aided transportation, while Italian authorities who continued to harbor Fascist sympathizers provided cover and help to those fleeing through their country.

Even the Vatican played a leading role in providing safe haven, with bishops such as the Austrian Alois Hudal, cited years later as a prominent figure from Rome, a fervent supporter of Hitler and his regime, and charged with supplying the necessary papers, false identification, and ultimately migration from Europe. As well as such seemingly pious assistance, ODESSA and those who sought their help would need places to resettle and that meant regimes which sympathized with Nazi policies and ideologies. Some South American leaders, most prominently Argentina's Juan Perón (aided by his country's

Catholic Church) were willing to help with the escape from Europe and facilitate new lives on their continent.

Notorious Nazis benefited from what became known as Perón's "Final Destination." Adolf Eichmann and Josef Mengele were just two of the high-level Nazis who fled across the Atlantic to start new lives in Argentina and Brazil respectively.

Popular culture and Hollywood (such as Frederick Forsyth's 1972 thriller *The Odessa Files*, made into a movie of the same name starring Jon Voight, and the high-profile 1978 *The Boys From Brazil*, starring Gregory Peck and Laurence Olivier) have kept the theory alive. While the world eventually moved on from the barbarity of the war, ODESSA helped too many Nazi criminals escape justice.

The Nazi doctor and war criminal, Josef Mengele (third from right), pictured at some time in the 1970s.

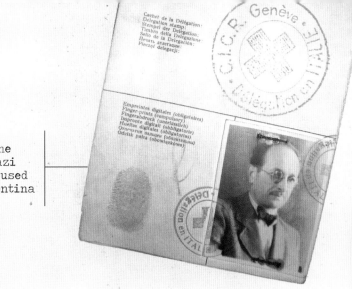

The Red Cross passport that the high-ranking Nazi Adolf Eichmann used to get into Argentina in 1950.

THE SKEPTICS

No one can argue that after the atrocities of the Second World War, as the world struggled to come to terms with the horror that was unfolding, members of Hitler's regime were aided and abetted in their quest to avoid capture. What many do question is whether one organization, that known among conspiracy theorists as ODESSA, was solely to blame for their disappearance. Instead, skeptics suggest that the idea of ODESSA simplified the argument, that those on both sides benefited from its existence.

Experts are in agreement that these routes, known as "ratlines," from Europe to the safety of South America or the Middle East were indeed set up using like-minded, powerful contacts (rather than an actual organized body) through Italy and Spain. Supporters of regimes such as that of Juan Perón in Argentina have long argued that they had nothing to do with the sanctuary being sought on their continent by former Nazis, arguing it was merely the former Allies, predominantly the United States, looking to delegitimize what they argued were extreme regimes.

But why would Nazi sympathizers and those who opposed their ideology both benefit from the theory that ODESSA did indeed exist? For pro-Nazis the notion that their all-powerful Reich had been defeated would not do, therefore the idea that they were still organized, ready to rise again, able to create what they saw as a "Fourth Reich" was empowering. For the rest of the world, the idea that a pro-Nazi organization could exist will never allow complacency to set in. If ODESSA were real and able to flourish, the consequences of it ever being given the opportunity to resurface are unthinkable.

FURTHER READING

Beckett, Lee. *I Just Can't Help Believin'… : Conspiracy Theory Book One – Elvis Presley*. Junction Publishing, 2020

Birnes, William J. *The Day After Roswell*. Gallery Books, 2017

Brotherton, Robert. *Suspicious Minds: Why We Believe Conspiracy Theories*. Bloomsbury, 2015

Cassam, Quassim. *Conspiracy Theories*. Polity, 2019

DiEugenio, James. *The JFK Assassination*. Skyhorse, 2018

Guyenot, Laurent. *JFK–9/11: 50 Years of Deep State*. Progressive Press, 2014

Hodapp, David & Von Kannon, Alice. *Conspiracy Theories and Secret Societies For Dummies*. For Dummies, 2008

King, Jamie. *Conspiracy Theories: A Compendium of History's Greatest Mysteries and More Recent Cover-Ups*. Summersdale Publishers, 2020

Landau, Elaine. *Osama bin Laden: The Life and Death of the 9/11 al-Qaeda Mastermind*. Twenty-First Century Books, 2013

Lewis, John E. *The Mammoth Book of Conspiracies*. Little Brown, 2012

Marrs, Jim. *Inside Job: Unmasking the 9/11 Conspiracies*. Origin Press, 2004

Marrs, Jim. *The Illuminati: The Secret Society that Hijacked the World*. Visible Ink Press, 2017

Mikovitz, Judy & Heckenlively, Kent. *Plague of Corruption: Restoring Faith in the Promise of Science*. Skyhorse, 2020

Moore, Fionnbarr. *RMS Lusitania: The Story of a Wreck*. Wordwell Books, 2020

River, Charles. *ODESSA: The Controversial History of the Mysterious Network that Helped Nazis Escape Germany after World War II*. Create Space, 2016

Shenon, Philip. *A Cruel and Shocking Act: The Secret History of the Kennedy Assassination.* Little Brown, 2015

Smith, Daniel. *100 Things They Don't Want You To Know: Conspiracies, Mysteries and Unsolved Crimes.* Quercus, 2017

Southwell, David. *Unsolved Celebrity Mysteries (Mysteries and Conspiracies).* Rosen Publishing Group, 2007

Weaver, Trevor. *Man On The Moon: Fact Or Fiction?* 2018

INDEX

PICTURE CREDITS

11: © John Mathew Smith & www.celebrity-photos.com / CC A-SA 2.0

12: © Pierre Boussel / Getty Images

14: © Anwar Hussein / Getty Images

15: © Langevin Jacques / Getty Images

18: © United Archives / Getty Images

19: © Olli Gill / CC A-SA 2.0

21: © Bettmann / Getty Images

22: © Adam Jones, Ph.D. / CC A-SA 3.0

23: © Daniel Schwen / CC A-SA 4.0

27: © Antonio Scorza / AFP via Getty Images

29: © Antonio Scorza / AFP via Getty Images

32: © Bettmann / Getty Images

37: © Photo 12 / Alamy Stock Photo

38: © Michael O'Neill / Corbis via Getty Images

39: © Ozier Muhammad / Newsday RM via Getty Images

40: © Javier Gonzalez Leyva / Shutterstock

43: © Michael Ochs Archive / Getty Images

45: © Warner Brothers / Getty Images

55: © Scott Barbour / Getty Images

56: © David Price / CC A-SA 2.0

57: © Alex Wong / Getty Images

59: © Ian Waldie / Getty Images

63: © LIG7AGR / Shutterstock

65: © Stefano Bianchetti / Corbis via Getty Images

67: © ra3rn / Shutterstock

69: © Movie Poster Image Art / Getty Images

71: © Dave Rushen / SOPA Images / LightRocket via Getty Images

74: © Jesus Abad-El Colombiano / AFP via Getty Images

75: © Bettmann / Getty Images

77: © Eric Vandeville / Gamma-Rapho via Getty Images

79: © Chip Somodevilla / Getty Images

81: © Rob Mieremet / CC0 1.0

85: © Strebe / CC A-SA 3.0

86: © Max Dallocco / Shutterstock

92: © Alex Wong / Getty Images

93: © Hamid Mir / CC A-SA 3.0

97: © Omer Messinger / Getty Images

101: © Shawn Thew / AFP via Getty Images

113: © Popperfoto via Getty Images

114: © Bettmann / Getty Images

115: © Shawshots / Alamy Stock Photo

128: © Roberto Stuckert Filho / PR / CC A-SA 2.5

133: © Media_works / Shutterstock

136: © Bektour / CC A-SA 3.0

138: © SAC Tim Laurence / MOD

139: © Getty Images

149: © UTA Library / CC A-SA 4.0

150: © UTA Library / CC A-SA 4.0

152: © Joshua Roberts / AFP via Getty Images

157: © Richard Mortel / CC A-SA 2.0

159: © Keystone-France / Gamma-Keystone via Getty Images

161: © Keystone-France / Gamma-Keystone via Getty Images

162: © Universal History Archive / Universal Images Group via Getty Images

163: © Bild 183-H1216-0500-002 / CC A-SA 3.0

165: © Fine Art Images / Heritage Images / Getty Images

176: © Christophel Fine Art / Universal Images Group via Getty Images

184: © Bettmann / Getty Images